About This Book

Why is this topic important?

Over half of all employees in today's world of work are under the age of forty. However, the majority of the professionals doing traditional stand-up delivery of workplace training today are in their forties, fifties, and pushing into their sixties! The basic approach of these maturing trainers to the design of training and their basic style of delivering that training has remained relatively unchanged over the years. Slowly, methodically, step-by-step, they tell, tell, tell and bore, bore, bore their younger learners. Unless they begin to make serious changes in the way they design and deliver training, their own effectiveness, credibility, and, ultimately, their employability will be damaged.

What can you achieve with this book?

How to Design and Deliver Training for the New and Emerging Generations is a survival guide for Boomer trainers who are encountering increasing numbers of younger learners in their classrooms. It contains realistic, non-threatening steps that you can take, techniques that you can use, and engaging games that you can easily incorporate into your training repertoire. This practical, innovative book helps Boomer trainers cut through the jungles of their own generational learning habits and clear a path to the new and emerging generations of learners.

How is this book organized?

Part One of the book presents information on the Baby Boomer generation and the generations that follow, compares the training habits of Boomer trainers and the learning style needs of younger learners, and then addresses five key needs of younger learners: pick up the pace, increase interaction, link to the learner, offer options, and make it fun. The last chapter rattles a few favorite training paradigms around time, space, and matter. Part One presents hundreds of tips, tricks, and simple techniques for designing and delivering training that will engage the younger learner.

Part Two of the book presents twenty games and structured activities that can be used with a variety of common training topics, all designed to address the five key needs of the younger learner, yet effective with any age group or mix of age groups.

About Pfeiffer

Pfeiffer serves the professional development and hands-on resource needs of training and human resource practitioners and gives them products to do their jobs better. We deliver proven ideas and solutions from experts in HR development and HR management, and we offer effective and customizable tools to improve workplace performance. From novice to seasoned professional, Pfeiffer is the source you can trust to make yourself and your organization more successful.

Essential Knowledge Pfeiffer produces insightful, practical, and comprehensive materials on topics that matter the most to training and HR professionals. Our Essential Knowledge resources translate the expertise of seasoned professionals into practical, how-to guidance on critical workplace issues and problems. These resources are supported by case studies, worksheets, and job aids and are frequently supplemented with CD-ROMs, websites, and other means of making the content easier to read, understand, and use.

Essential Tools Pfeiffer's Essential Tools resources save time and expense by offering proven, ready-to-use materials—including exercises, activities, games, instruments, and assessments—for use during a training or team-learning event. These resources are frequently offered in looseleaf or CD-ROM format to facilitate copying and customization of the material.

Pfeiffer also recognizes the remarkable power of new technologies in expanding the reach and effectiveness of training. While e-hype has often created whizbang solutions in search of a problem, we are dedicated to bringing convenience and enhancements to proven training solutions. All our e-tools comply with rigorous functionality standards. The most appropriate technology wrapped around essential content yields the perfect solution for today's on-the-go trainers and human resource professionals.

Pfeiffer
www.pfeiffer.com

Susan El-Shamy

How to Design and Deliver Training for the New and Emerging Generations

Pfeiffer
A Wiley Imprint
www.pfeiffer.com

Library of Congress Cataloging-in-Publication Data
El-Shamy, Susan.
  How to design and deliver training for the new and emerging
generations / Susan El-Shamy.
    p. cm.
Includes bibliographical references (p. 175).
  ISBN 0-7879-6977-X (alk. paper)
  1. Employees—Training of. 2. Employees—Training of—Problems,
exercises, etc. I. Title.
  HF5549.5.T7E423 2004
  658.3'12404—dc22   2003025430

Acquiring Editor: Martin Delahoussaye
Director of Development: Kathleen Dolan Davies
Production Editor: Nina Kreiden
Editor: Rebecca Taff
Manufacturing Supervisor: Bill Matherly

Editorial Assistant: Laura Reizman
Interior Design: Gene Crofts
Cover Design: Chris Wallace
Illustrations: Richard Sheppard Illustration
             Lotus Art

Printed in the United States of America
Printing 10 9 8 7 6 5 4 3 2 1

Contents

part TWO

Games 73

CD Contents

Games and Activities

1 Sculpt Away
2 Word Search Mania
3 One Hundred Ways
4 A Matter of Definition
5 A Change of View
6 Royal Flush
7 Hunt for Examples
8 Two-Card Audit
9 Walk the Talk
10 Find the Top Ten
11 The Whole Is Greater
12 A Stick by Any Other Name
13 Online Treasure Hunt
14 Generational Bingo
15 Q&A Black Jack
16 Approach and Coach
17 Ready, Set, Goal
18 Involve to Solve
19 Across the Board
20 Jelly Bean Art

Introduction

Have you ever had that nightmare? You know, the one where you're attending a training session that is being delivered by someone from an older generation. You nod politely as the graying trainer begins the lecture with an outdated example from a long-gone era. You sigh quietly as you hear the story of the two frogs that fell into the container of cream. You glance at your watch as the trainer searches through a large three-ring binder to find the appropriate overhead transparency, and then, as the mature figure walks around the room, reading from the material on the screen, you find yourself checking your watch again. As the lights dim for the talking-head video, you notice the flashing message on your pager: *Wake up! It's not too late!* And then you do wake up and you realize that the trainer in the dream is you!

Frightening, isn't it? How did it happen? Not too long ago we were the up-and-coming corporate trainers. Fast and funky, cool and clever, always a step ahead, we wowed them with experiential learning. We held up mirrors with magic letters like ESTJ and ENTP. We made team building happen, man.

We kept up with the times. We managed change. We made the transition to Power-Point. We got online. Why, we even designed e-learning programs. So what happened?

We got older; that's what happened. And "they" got younger. And that's the way of the world. But it's not too late to wake up and make a few changes. And that's what this book is all about.

How to Design and Deliver Training for the New and Emerging Generations is a survival guide for Baby Boomer trainers who are encountering increasing numbers of younger learners in their classrooms. The U.S. Bureau of Statistics reports that over 45 percent of today's workforce is under the age of forty. And when these younger workers show up for workplace training programs, whom do they find teaching the program? Trainers from their parents' generation. Yes, indeed. The majority of us professionals doing the stand-up delivery of corporate training today are in our forties, fifties, and pushing into our sixties! The American Society for Training and Development, with a membership of almost 70,000 training professionals, lists over 70 percent of its members as over the age of forty. Thirty-five percent are over fifty!

Now, of course, there are younger trainers out there, and many of them don't belong to ASTD, just as many older trainers don't. But still, the chances are quite high that the majority of corporate training decision-makers and senior trainers are from the Baby Boom generation. And we Boomers certainly influence the design and, to a great extent, the delivery style of a major portion of workplace training. Consequently, we have a large number of Boomer Generation designers and deliverers of training programs who are designing for and delivering to a growing number of younger learners from the emerging generations.

"So what?" you might ask. Why is this a problem? Well, to begin with, the basic approach to the design and delivery of training that we Boomer trainers have developed, adhered to, and passed along over the years is very structured, step-by-step, lecture-dominated, text-oriented, criterion-referenced, and often more focused on how we enjoy teaching rather than on how the learner enjoys learning. When learners from the new and emerging generations encounter our tried-and-true programs and approaches, they often leave expressing the need for training programs that are faster and more flexible, multi-optioned, interaction-dominated, visually oriented, more fun, and more involving. And that's a problem.

Younger learners are not overtly rebellious. They don't gripe and complain to Boomer trainers or to their management. They just tune out, leave early, and avoid future "old-timer" training programs. Unless we Boomer trainers begin to address the needs of these younger learners and make serious changes in the way we design and deliver training, our effectiveness in the classroom, our credibility within our profession, and, ultimately, our employability will be severely damaged.

● ●

SO WHAT'S A BOOMER TO DO?

How to Design and Deliver Training for the New and Emerging Generations has been written to raise awareness regarding the needs of younger learners and to help trainers of all ages make the changes necessary to address those needs. These emerging-generation learners require a different type of training design and delivery, and this book covers five essential changes that Boomers must make to be more effective trainers and meet the needs of their younger customers: pick up the pace of the training, increase interaction, link to our learners, offer more options and choices within our programs, and make our training more fun. To help you address these five needs and make the essential changes required, this book contains hundreds of realistic, nonthreatening steps that you can take, techniques that you can use, and engaging games that you can easily incorporate into your training repertoire. They are appropriate for use in all types of training programs, with all types of companies and organizations, and they can be used effectively with learners of all ages.

This book is written as a handbook, a survival guide, and contains a number of quizzes, charts, checklists, and things to do. Throughout the book you will find a running callout box called "The Nitty Gritty" that provides you with some very practical information regarding training resources and tools. *How to Design and Deliver Training for the New and Emerging Generations* is a resource that you can read from cover to cover or that you can randomly access and refer to as needed.

This survival guide is not only directed to mature training professionals, but to the younger training professionals among us who have been coached and developed by us Boomer trainers to do training the right way—the Boomer way. Regardless of where you fall on the generational continuum, if you are using the approaches and techniques developed and established in the seventies and eighties and still held tightly in place into the new millennium, this book is for you.

The book is divided into two parts. Part One presents information on the Baby Boom generation and the generations that follow and considers the learning differences among the generations. Next, we take a look at five key needs of younger learners—speed, interaction, relevancy, options, and fun—and present hundreds of ideas, tips, and techniques for designing and delivering training to address those key needs. Finally, some of the established paradigms regarding the time, space, and matter of training are questioned and suggestions are made for all-the-time, all-the-space-every-place, and all-that-matters learning.

Throughout Part One you will find an alarm clock icon used to indicate a dozen "wake-up calls" of important information or actions to take. So, if you only have time to check out a few key items of information or things to do, look for the wake-up call icons.

In Part One, you will also find quotes and comments from young people expressing their thoughts and ideas on how to make traditional workplace training and development programs more appealing to the younger generations. In my own quest to better understand the design and delivery of training for the emerging generations, I first read as much as I could of what was being written about these generations. Then I decided to survey a number of young people who were members of the emerging generations. In my surveys (See Appendix), I asked them about the areas of learning differences regarding pace, interaction, relevancy, choices, and fun. I also asked them to describe their ideal educational class or seminar, to list the qualities and characteristics of their ideal instructor, and to tell me about the things that they have most liked and disliked about the classes, workshops, and seminars that they have taken.

I also held a focus group with some dynamic graduate students in telecommunications at Indiana University, where I listened to their critiques and experiences with Baby Boom trainers. I gathered their thoughts and ideas on how to make traditional workplace training and development programs more appealing to the younger generations. It was an enlightening experience.

Part Two of this book contains twenty games and structured activities designed to address the five key needs of the younger learner. These games and activities have been tested with a variety of learners and can be used in a variety of training programs with any type of company or organization. They can also be adapted for use in a wide range of programs. To give some idea of the application possibilities for the games, I have used a running example throughout the games sections, and, for each game, I have included an example of how that particular game might be used in a standard team-building program.

There is also a small icon included with each game that indicates the extent to which that game addresses each of the five needs: pick up the pace, increase interaction, link to the learner, offer options, and make it fun. You will also find a number of "Nitty-Gritty" callout boxes in the game section with information on where to find certain items, suggestions for prizes, pertinent websites, and so forth. Although all twenty games and activities address the five key needs of younger learners, they were also designed to captivate and educate learners of all ages.

So turn down the Golden Oldies, put on your glasses, get out a yellow highlighter, and explore the ideas, techniques, and fabulous games and activities that lie ahead.

part ONE

The Different Needs of Younger Learners

The first part of this book addresses the issues and problems confronting Baby Boomer trainers who are encountering increasing numbers of younger learners in their classrooms. If you are doing Boomer-style training for participants from younger generations with different learning styles and different learning needs, then tune in to the suggestions, tips, and techniques in the following chapters. They can help you cut through the tangle of your own generational learning habits and clear a path to the new and emerging generations of learners.

The Boomers and the Generations That Follow

The Baby Boomers are those seventy-seven million Americans born between 1946 and 1964 who have dominated American culture for the past fifty years. Born in the years following World War II and growing up during the optimistic fifties when the nation enjoyed unparalleled prosperity and economic expansion, the Boomer generation has left its mark on every facet of American society. Ken Dychtwald, in *Age Power*, describes the Boomer generation as not just populating life stages or consumer trends, but transforming them in new directions. For example, he writes that Boomers "didn't just date, they transformed sex roles and practices." They didn't just "go to the doctor, they transformed healthcare" (Dychtwald, 1999, p. 69).

In general Boomers are said to be positive, hard-working, and future-oriented. However, researchers point out differences in Boomer characteristics between those born early in the Boomer time period, say 1945 to 1955, and those who came along later, between 1955 and 1965. In *Generations at Work,* Zemke, Raines, and Filipczak describe early Boomers as "more idealistic, more likely to be workaholics, and more likely to have put career first," whereas they depict Boomers born later in the Baby Boomer time period as not identifying as much with the 1960s and being a bit more "laid back and cynical" (Zemke, Raines, Filipczak, 2000, p. 71).

Regardless of some differences in younger and older Boomers, the sheer numbers of the Boomer generation have caused them to wield a major impact on all aspects of American culture, including the workplace and the field of training and development. This huge population has pursued self-understanding and self-fulfillment and, some might say, self-gratification. They value health, wellness, and spirituality. And many of these aspects of Boomer culture have left their mark on the design and delivery of workplace training.

For the past number of years, many of us Boomers have begun to notice the rising numbers of younger people coming into their own in our wake. These emerging generations may be our younger brothers and sisters, they may be our children, even our grandchildren, but there they are—almost 130 million members of the emerging generations ages four to forty. As more and more is being written about these newer generations, various titles and different defining time periods are being used.

● ●

GENERATION X

You may be most familiar with the term Generation X, used for that generation of about fifty million who were born between 1965 and 1976. Because this generation followed the Baby Boomer generation and is smaller in number, it has also been referred to as the Baby Busters. In the introduction to his book *Welcome to the Jungle,* Geoffrey T. Holtz describes Generation X as "Born just after the magnificent baby boom, we are forever cast in the shadow of that pig-in-the-python that has dominated our nation's attention from its members' sheer numbers. . . . In the wake of this group, we have often had to fight to be noticed at all, let along to be judged by fair standards or understood" (Holtz, 1995, p. 1).

Perhaps the most maligned and misunderstood of the emerging generations, people born early in the Generation X time period had to put up with that wretched term "slackers," and their hesitation and distrust of society caused them to be labeled as cynical, lazy, and ungrateful. To add to their irritation, older Generation Xers watched younger members of their generation become super-techies and, for a few years anyway, enjoy the benefits of the dot.com revolution. On March 1, 2000, Salon.com ran an incredibly funny and insightful feature by Jim Rasenberger entitled, "My Generation Sucks!" Rasenberger, a late Boomer/early Generation Xer, mockingly describes what he calls "genvy" or gen-envy of his age group toward the twenty-somethings, saying, "under those mopey expressions, it turns out, were the toothy smiles of Internet tycoons" (Rasenberger, 2000).

Time, of course, and the fall of so many dot.coms, has taken care of some of that "genvy," but the second half of Generation X have enjoyed being part of the information technology explosion and their knowledge, skills, and high comfort levels with technology have made them valuable employees. Overall, Generation X workers are seen as not only technology literate, but also as creative and adaptable. However, they are said to require "flexible hours, an informal work environment, and hands-off supervision" (Zemke, Raines, Filipczak, 2000, p. 111).

● ●

THE YOUNGEST OF THE EMERGING GENERATIONS

The youngest of the emerging generations were born between 1977 and the present. A variety of terminology and time periods are presently being used for this youngest of the emerging generations. Don Tapscott, in his excellent work *Growing Up Digital,* uses the term "Net Generation" or "N-Gen" for those eighty million–plus young people born between 1977 and 1997 (Tapscott, 1998, p. 1).

Mark Prensky, in *Digital Game-Based Learning,* uses the term "Games Generation," and sometimes the term "Nintendo Generation"; but Prensky gives no specific birth years for those included in the Games Generation (Prensky, 2001, p. 35). Neil Howe and William Strauss, in their book *Millennials Rising,* use the term "Millennials" for those 76 million children born between 1982 and 2000 (Howe & Strauss, 2000, p. 4). (The year 1982 is the birth year of students who graduated from high school in the year 2000.)

The authors of *Generations at Work* broadened and overlapped some of the years defining the various generations, factoring in what they term "the feel" of the generations. For the youngest of the emerging generations, they use the term "Nexters" (Zemke, Raines, Filipczak, 2000, p. 40). There are other terms in use for this newest generation, including "Digital Generation," "Generation Why," "Generation Y" (as differentiated from Generation X), and the "E-Generation." I've also seen the term "Netters" for those in the Net Generation and "Echo Boomers" for the children of the Boomers. It's not clear yet which label will eventually stick, but one of them surely will.

Regardless of what you call them, the oldest members of this very youngest of the generations have been graduating from college in the last few years, and many are entering the full-time workforce. And there are hundreds of thousands of them working at part-time jobs across the nation as they go to school. In terms of work, the Millennials, or the Net Generation, are seen as "optimistic, independent yet good at collaboration, technologically savvy, and good at multi-tasking" (Tapscott, 1998, p. 211).

And eighty million is no small number. This generation by any name will be influential on American culture. Their ease and expertise with all things digital, their global world view, and their propensity for multi-tasking will make an impact on the world of work and, in turn, the world of training and development.

● ●

GENERATIONAL PROFILES

When I combine information from the various resources above and from my own surveys and experiences to produce an overview of the profiles of these generations as potential trainers, it looks something like this:

The Generations as Potential Trainers

BOOMER TRAINERS

- Born between 1945 and 1965

- Belong to ASTD and read *Training & Development Journal* and *Training* magazine

- Value hard work, involvement, and "personal growth"

- Tend to be optimistic, positive, and look for the good in situations

- Enjoy the spotlight and being in charge of the show

- Like to be up-to-date and "in the know"

- Have some technical "know how" and experience, but fear still lurks

EMERGING GENERATIONS

- Generation X Trainers

  - Born between 1965 and 1977

  - May not belong to ASTD; may read *Training* magazine; read *Wired, Fast Company, Real Simple,* and visit Salon.com

  - Value independence and self-reliance and often question authority

  - Tend to be skeptical, questioning, but not afraid of risk

  - Do not like the spotlight, but like to have control of things

  - Are at ease with, and very proficient with, technology

- Net Generation Trainers

  ▶ Born between 1977 and 1997

  ▶ May never have heard of ASTD; Read Harry Potter, *Teen Magazine,* and online web comics at penny-arcade.com

  ▶ Value achievement, diversity, and collaboration

  ▶ Are globally aware and globally connected

  ▶ Technology is a natural part of life

● ●

DO THE GENERATIONS LEARN DIFFERENTLY?

When it comes to generational differences, training and development professionals are naturally interested in learning styles. Are there really differences in learning styles and approaches to information gathering and problem solving among the generations? You bet there are.

Watch any transgenerational group approach to gathering information and see what happens. Holidays present good opportunities for spotting generational learning differences. The day after Christmas someone suggests that the whole group go to a movie. Everyone agrees wholeheartedly and starts looking for the movie listings. Grandma digs through the stack of newspapers looking for the entertainment section. Mom grabs the phone, a pencil, and paper, and dials the local Cineplex. Junior goes online and gets the local listings. And cousin Sally pulls out her combination PDA-pager and punches the cinema icon.

Observe learners of different ages researching a topic. In general, Boomers prefer to read about the topic. They go through a few basic printed resources on the subject, taking notes, marking passages, and making outlines. They may turn to professional journals and respected magazines to read the latest that has been written on the subject. They go to bookstores and libraries to see "what's out there" on the topic.

Although they will also read on the topic, learners from Generation X are more likely to start with the Internet, accessing search engine services and visiting a variety of sites on the subject. They will check out printed resources online, and if they decide to read a book on the topic, there is a good chance they will read the reviews of that book online, check the card files of their local library online to see if the book is available, and if need be, purchase the book online.

The younger Generation X learner and the Millennial learner, while also using the Internet, will often prefer to delve into the subject matter in a more personal and interactive manner. They might broadcast an electronic appeal for information to various friends and e-mail contacts or they might post inquiries on electronic bulletin boards. Whatever they do, they will do most of it electronically, simultaneously, and quickly.

● ●

THE TECHNOLOGICAL DIVIDE

Younger learners from Generation X (born between 1965 and 1980) and the Millennial Generation (born between 1980 and 2000) grew up learning to learn with Big Bird and Bert and Ernie. Their learning encounters were reinforced with sound and color and humor. They have been conditioned over their early learning years to respond to a different set of learning circumstances. As toddlers they played electronic learning games and, by age seven, eight, or nine, they moved on to Nintendo and a wide variety of fast-paced, increasingly sophisticated, video and computer games.

Members of these emerging generations had computers in their classrooms at school. (When did you first encounter a computer?) While older Generation Xers may not have had computers until high school or college, younger Generation Xers probably had them in grade school, definitely had them in high school, and couldn't survive without them in college. And most Millennials have never known a life without computers. In fact, many Millennials learned to keyboard before they learned to write.

The use of the Internet for communicating, learning, retrieving information, and accessing entertainment is a way of life for most of Generation X and the Millennials. And consider all the other electronic aids and gadgets that are a part of, and have always been a part of, the younger generations' lifestyle. These include cell phones, pagers, PDAs, Ipods, GameBoys, and a multitude of electronic game paraphernalia.

Now we Boomers use computers and surf the net, we seldom go anywhere without our cell phones and/or pagers, and the younger Boomers among us can be seen with personal digital assistants (PDAs) and digital cameras. But our use of technology in the classroom is minimal. The most that many of us Boomer-age trainers have done to keep up with technology in the classroom is to transfer the information on our overhead transparencies to multicolored PowerPoint presentations. Our basic approach to the design of training, and our basic style of delivering that training, has remained relatively unchanged in terms of actually using technology in the classroom to any great extent.

GAME–PLAYING HABITS OF THE YOUNGER GENERATIONS

Research conducted in 2002 by the Interactive Digital Software Association looked into the computer game–playing habits of U.S. residents age six and over and found that more than 50 percent play computer games. The same research reports that there were over 221 million computer and video games sold in the United States in 2002, amounting to sales of over $6.9 billion (IDSA, 2003). Now that's a lot of computer games, a lot of money, and a lot of game playing, and it does have its effects.

Game playing does not diminish as members of the emerging generations go off to college. In a recent report on college students' use of video, computer, and online games, it was reported that 70 percent of college students play video, computer, or online games at least once in a while and that 65 percent report being regular or at least occasional game players (Jones, 2003, p. 6).

When you combine the ongoing game playing habits of younger learners with their constant use of computers and the Internet, along with their use of all the other digital electronic devices their lives embrace, there is bound to be an effect on how they prefer to learn, on how they learn best, and on how they are most comfortable learning. Mark Prensky describes our younger current workers and all of our future workers as "being raised with a very different set—a digital set—of key formative experiences" (Prensky, 2001, p. 38). Doesn't it follow that these digital, key formative experiences will impact the receptivity, the readiness, to use the psychological term, that these learners bring to a learning situation? Workplace designers and deliverers of training must address these unique needs.

HOW IMPORTANT ARE
GENERATIONAL LEARNING DIFFERENCES?

At first, it is appealing to dismiss the generational gap between trainers and trainees as no big deal. In fact, isn't that the way it has always been, those doing the teaching are older, and supposedly wiser, than those taking the training? The answer, of course, is "yes, but." Yes, in general there has often been an age difference between those teaching and those being taught, especially when we are young. But as adults, we begin to find ourselves in learning situations where the age differences lessen and, particularly in technical fields, we Baby Boomer members of the workforce may have found ourselves learning computer programming, web design, and other technical topics from instructors the age of our children. And who among us has not called on our children, perhaps even our grandchildren, to explain a newfangled feature of our latest software upgrade or to get us back in the world of the living after our computer has crashed?

But when it comes to nontechnical training, when it comes to the design and delivery of standard employee development training programs, the majority of the trainers at the front of the classroom will be from the Baby Boomer generation. And for the most part, we are knowledgeable, competent, hardworking, and skilled at what we do. We know our content, and over the years we have developed effective means of delivering that content.

But as the number of younger learners increases in the corporate classroom, many of our tried-and-true approaches to designing and delivering training will need to be changed, updated, and, occasionally, overhauled entirely in order to be effective with the younger generations. And I'm not referring to changing generational reference points and outdated examples, although these are important. I'm talking about addressing these digital, key formative experiences that have affected the learning styles and overall approaches to learning of the younger generations—even generational differences in cognitive development.

● ●

GENERATIONAL DIFFERENCES IN COGNITIVE DEVELOPMENT

Contrary to long-held beliefs that all humans follow the same basic thought processes, Dr. Richard Nisbett and his colleagues at the University of Michigan have done research in the last few years that shows that "people who grow up in different cultures do not just think about different things: they think differently"(Goode, 2000, p. 1). Basically, Nisbett and his colleagues argue that "cognitive processes are far more malleable than mainstream Western psychology has assumed" (Goode, 2000, p. 1).

Their research upholds what anthropologists, social psychologists, and individuals who have lived for long periods of time in cultures very different from their own have described. There are cultural differences to be sure, but these differences may be caused by differences in actual mental processes. If this is so, that the cultural environment strongly influences, perhaps even shapes, our "habits of thought—the strategies people adopt in processing information and making sense of the world around them" (Goode, 2000)—then it holds to reason that the younger generation's use of video games and other electronic media from a very early age may have affected their mental, and certainly their social, habits of taking in and processing information.

The question for Boomer designers and deliverers of training is, "What are we going to do about it?"

Training the Different Generations

Most adults have a basic learning style reflective of how they were taught in school. We adapt a bit to new technologies, we incorporate a few new approaches, but by and large, we are most comfortable with learning approaches not too different from those used to teach us when we were young. And teaching methods have changed dramatically over the past thirty years. If the last time you were in a public school classroom was well before 1980, or even 1990, check things out. The look, style, and approaches to learning have changed.

Many young people from the emerging generations grew up with learning approaches that used teamwork and collaboration. They learned to use critical thinking skills. They thrived in classrooms with learning pods and subject corners and individualized options. They took part in engaged learning projects. According to the North Central Regional Education Laboratory (NCRL) and the Stanford Research Institute (SRI), engaged learning, problem-based-learning, and self-directed learning are all terms used for "teaching philosophies that encourage the development of autonomous learners who are motivated to become, and responsible for being, in control of their own learning processes" (www.ncrel.org).

What about Baby Boomers and our learning style? Our learning came through lectures and printed text with an occasional opportunity to do something. Our public school classrooms of the fifties and sixties were sparse, strict, and structured. Teachers taught, reading assignments were given, and things were done sequentially.

Many of us were in college in the sixties, and while some may have been marching and protesting outside of class, in class we all listened up and took good notes. In the seventies, concerned with inner peace, human growth, and reaching our full potential, we sat in circles on beanbags sharing our feelings and letting it all hang out. We looked to gurus and subject-matter experts to tell us the answers—or at least provide insights. We were inundated with self-help books and self-development seminars (remember TA workshops and est seminars?).

● ●

THE BOOMER STYLE OF TRAINING

As for those Baby Boomers who became trainers and designers of training, we learned to value personal growth, to share our personal experiences, and therefore we often invite trainees to do the same. Many Boomers approach training as much as a growth experience as a learning experience. We are often concerned for the psychic comfort of our charges.

As an example, take the "set-up" of a training program. If you've been doing training like I have for the past twenty years, the first thirty minutes of your program may be carefully devoted to setting a good training climate—welcoming participants, making introductory remarks, presenting an overview of the class and its purpose and goals, covering housekeeping issues, and, of course, introducing yourself and then having the participants meet one another (preferably in a short, clever activity). All of this is done at an energetic, but evenly paced, tempo—accompanied by the appropriate distribution of three-ring binders, of course, and a sprinkling of overhead transparencies or colorful slides.

This approach to setting a good learning climate was established years ago, probably to deal with reluctant participants, many of whom were not happy about attending training. The idea behind the approach may have been to allay participant fears, establish the credentials of the presenter, reassure participants of the value of the course content, and put class members at ease with one another. This style may be very reassuring to older participants, as well as satisfying to our own "encounter group" roots, but to many younger participants, it is frustratingly slow, a little too personal, and seems quite unnecessary.

YOUNGER LEARNER NEEDS NOT BEING MET

Various researchers and observers of the younger generations have itemized differences among the generations that call for new approaches to teaching and training. Mark Prensky, in *Digital Game-Based Learning,* lists numerous ways the Games Generation is different, including their need for speed, connectivity, and activity, and their capacity to randomly access and parallel process a variety of information simultaneously. Prensky writes, "So, in the end, it is all these cognitive differences, resulting from years of 'new media socialization' and profoundly affecting and changing the generations' learning styles and abilities, that cry out for new approaches to learning . . ." (p. 65).

Don Tapscott, in *Growing Up Digital,* writes, "By exploiting the digital media, educators and students can shift to a new, more powerful, and more effective learning paradigm" (Tapscott, 1998, p. 142). The new paradigm he discusses includes such things as a more interactive and nonsequential access to information, more customized learning, and a move toward learning as fun. In her article "The Young and the Rest of Us: Should Trainers Tailor Their Technique Depending on the Age of the Audience?" written after interviewing a variety of trainers about their interactions with younger-generation learners, Jennifer Salopek writes, "Younger workers like to learn at their own pace, need much interactivity, and want to keep updating their skills—constantly" (Salopek, 2000).

When discussing the work ethics of Generation X workers, Zemke, Raines, and Filipczak advise, "Don't look through the traditional lens. You won't find it. If you want to tap into it, give them a lot to do and some freedom regarding how the work gets done. You'll be surprised how much these 'slackers' can accomplish and still walk out the door at 5:00 P.M." (2000, p. 111). This advice also works well for the design of training.

WHAT YOUNGER LEARNERS SAY THEY NEED

When I asked younger learners to describe their ideal educational class or seminar in the surveys I conducted, they made comments like:

- "It would involve a variety of activities and move at a fairly rapid pace."

- "It would use interactive learning and technology."

- "Use technology to enhance learning!"

● "Make it fast-paced with lots of chances to apply what we are learning."

● "The best seminar would have lots of video games, prizes, interaction with all the people at the seminar, and candy."

● "I have rarely enjoyed a seminar where the instructor simply stands and talks. Bring in examples, video clips, media, something that helps students learn and keeps them from falling asleep or letting their minds wander."

● "I want a lot of hands-on in a workshop. The more I can work with what I'm learning, the more I'll take with me and remember afterwards."

● "The challenge for content developers is to find something that makes people think of the subject matter in a different way than they do. Take something outside of their regular paradigm and say here is another example of this from a movie—or a video clip, something popular. It engages the mind right away."

Did you find yourself assessing your own programs as you read through these quotes above?

● ●

WHAT DO BOOMER TRAINERS NEED TO DO?

If one compares the learning habits and preferences of the younger, emerging generations with the teaching habits and preferences of the older, Boomer teachers and trainers, a few key needs of the younger learners emerge—needs that can be easily met in the design and delivery of almost any training program to make it more appealing to younger learners. Think of these five needs as antidotes to five unfortunate habits of well-meaning Boomer trainers. Let's take a look at these unfortunate habits and the effects they have on younger learners.

Boomers tend to use a leisurely, even pace when they train. We do not consider this pace to be slow, by no means. And we do vary our pace and are often energetic. Younger learners, however, are accustomed to a much faster, more driving pace. And when they are forced to slow down, they become bored.

Boomer trainers use a predominantly telling style and are still very text-oriented. It's hard for us to feel comfortable unless we have passed out lots of printed material and gone over it, and perhaps gone over it again, verbally. Younger learners are more accustomed to visual examples, less text, and less telling. Again, too much telling turns them off, and their minds wander. They may even pull out a GameBoy to get them through the lecture. They have a great need for interactivity.

"Cover the content" may be the mantra of many a Boomer trainer. We Boomers feel a great need to cover the content because our success as trainers has often been measured by the ability of our participants to test well on the content, thus proving that learning has occurred. Younger learners are more concerned that the material or content is relevant to them and their situations. If it's not interesting or relevant to them, if there has been no link made to their lives and their needs, they tune out. What often amazes us older trainers is that younger learners can seem to be spacing out, paying no attention to our telling, perhaps even doing something else, and still do well on the test!

Boomer trainers are unrelentingly guided by the very linear course outline and course design. Again, this very linear approach is very different from the constant multiple options that digital learners are accustomed to. Having little choice and no options, no deviations from the agenda, no unpredictable spurts of unexpected information, the younger learner is again fighting boredom.

And finally, we come to fun. Boomers are not against fun. We love a good time, and we sprinkle a fair amount of fun here and there in our training programs. But when younger learners say they want the learning to be fun, they want all kinds of things: more interaction, more incentives, more involvement, more challenge—both physical and mental.

Put all of these needs and habits together and what do you get? A dynamic that pushes the learner away instead of pulling the learner in.

BOOMER HABITS	YOUNGER LEARNER NEEDS
Use a leisurely, even pace	Pick up the pace
Use telling, text-oriented methods	Increase interaction
Focus on the content	Link to the learner
Take a linear approach	Offer options
Employ a prudent amount of fun	Make learning fun

In the next few chapters, we will take a look at each of these five younger-learner needs and suggest ways of addressing them in the design and delivery of training. Meanwhile, why not see how you do on an assessment of the push and pull between the generations, presented in Exhibit 2.1.

EXHIBIT 2.1. Hey, You're Losing Me, Dude

Is your training losing the emerging generations? Take this short assessment and find out.

Directions: Circle a number for each of the statements below according to how descriptive each statement is of you and your training. Use the following scale.

2 = Always   1 = Sometimes   0 = Never

1. I start my training programs with an immediate, dynamic activity.   2   1   0

2. In general, I maintain a lively, quick pace when I do training.   2   1   0

3. I give exact time limits for group activities and stick to them.   2   1   0

4. I present information in chunks and never reveal information one bit
    or line at a time.   2   1   0

5. I do not stand in front of overheads, flip charts, or PowerPoint presen-
    tations and read the content out loud.   2   1   0

6. My programs contain many opportunities for participants to interact.   2   1   0

7. I keep my lecturing and telling to a real minimum in my programs.   2   1   0

8. I incorporate "discovery learning" activities into all my training.   2   1   0

9. My programs contain many involving games and simulations.   2   1   0

10. Participants get up, move around, and do things often in my classes.   2   1   0

11. I include examples and illustrations from the popular culture of all the
    generations present in class.   2   1   0

12. I make use of a variety of electronic technologies in all my classes.   2   1   0

13. I use a great many visuals and graphics in my training.   2   1   0

14. I stimulate the senses of learners in my classes.   2   1   0

15. I let the learners generate the issues and problems they want to work
    on in my classes.   2   1   0

2 = Always   1 = Sometimes   0 = Never

16.	I give participants choices on how they accomplish class goals.	2	1	0
17.	The games and activities I use include lots of choices for the learner.	2	1	0
18.	I customize the structure and content of class according to the needs of the participants.	2	1	0
19.	Participants in my courses choose from simultaneous learning options.	2	1	0
20.	I am really not very linear in how I approach my training.	2	1	0
21.	I use themes for my programs and in-class games and activities.	2	1	0
22.	I give awards and prizes in my classes.	2	1	0
23.	My classes have lots of fun games and activities in them.	2	1	0
24.	I go out of my way to create a relaxed, pleasant learning environment.	2	1	0
25.	There is laughter and a good flow of energy in my classes.	2	1	0

Scoring

Now go through your answers and add up the numbers that you have circled. Write your total score on the line below. Then check the interpretation information below.

Total Score: _____

Interpretation

41 to 50	=	Excellent	*Way to go. Maybe you can still pick up a tip or two.*
31 to 40	=	Good	*But there is still some room for improvement.*
21 to 30	=	Not too bad	*But you've got work to do.*
11 to 20	=	Pretty bad	*Better start making some changes soon.*
0 to 10	=	Awful!	*You're losing them, Dude. You better get busy right NOW.*

● ●

TRAINING A MIX OF GENERATIONS

Although there may be particular workplace programs and special subjects that are targeted to specific age groups and certain work groups or job classifications may have higher representation of one age group or another, most training classes in the workplace will contain participants from all generations. The first step necessary to make the design and delivery of training to a class of mixed-generation participants as effective as possible is awareness.

Just realizing that a variety of techniques and approaches will be needed to fully engage such a class is important. The second step is to have the flexibility and willingness to adapt as you go and as needed. Finally, you will want to have available the necessary repertoire of techniques, games, and activities to utilize.

Emerging-generation techniques can work for everyone. However, it may be necessary to adjust the amount of such techniques and the extent to which you utilize them according to the individual class or program. If you consider the five younger generation's needs—pick up the pace, increase interactions, link to the learner, offer options, and turn up the fun factor—all can be effective with older learners. It is probably more a matter of degree. An extremely fast-paced program, with constant choices and simultaneous offerings, numerous group problem-solving activities, the use of high-tech, fantasy themes, games galore, and lots of incentives may prove a bit overwhelming and distracting to some Boomer learners, but then again, many may just learn to love it!

Ease Up on Boomer Habits with Mixed Generations

It also helps to be aware of your own generational manifestations. Remember the habits of Boomer trainers that younger learners don't like—talk too much, go too slow, step-by-step, and not much fun? Cutting back on some of these tendencies can be a useful first step to take. For example, if you're a Boomer trainer who talks too much, who loves to tell, explain, and lecture away, it would behoove you to find ways to cut way back on this tendency and talk less!

This isn't easy, I know. I'm such a Boomer trainer. There is nothing quite so enchanting as the sound of my own voice floating over an audience of attentive learners. But are they really attentive, or are they merely waiting for me to stop talking so we can get on to *doing* something? I think the voice of one Generation X graduate student running through my mind has helped me with my problem of talking too much. When asked to describe the worst instructors in the world, she sighed and muttered, "People who are talking to hear themselves talk."

Provide Some Cross-Generational Awareness

There may be times during training programs when it will be appropriate and helpful to include a little cross-generational learning; that is, give the learners information about generational differences and perhaps have an activity that illustrates their generational differences. For example, if you have a very wide range of ages in a particular class and you notice some mild generational conflicts, stop and talk about it. Try an activity like Generational Bingo (Activity 14 in Part Two of this book), which has participants interacting across generations and brings up generational differences in a fun way.

Raising awareness of generational differences, recognizing the perceptions and assumptions that generations have about one another, and discussing related issues could all be beneficial to the effectiveness of the training program and to cross-generational relationships in the workplace. For example, use a variety of examples and illustrations in order to appeal to different generations. Explain that you are doing so and let the participants share information with each other. For example, if you use one example from "Hill Street Blues" and second example from "Dawson's Creek" and you see a few bewildered looks, ask participants to explain the examples to each other.

Recognize and Respect All Generations

It is important that trainers of any age give respect and attention to all generations. Joking and teasing members of one generation or another is not a good thing to do. We must also be careful of generalizing and making assumptions due to age and generation. Many members of the Baby Boomer generation are technically savvy, and I'm sure there are younger learners out there who are not particularly technically competent. And that goes for all the traits assigned to the different generations.

Although it may be a good thing to recognize and discuss generational differences, it is not healthy and appropriate to overdo the labeling of people and generations. People don't like to be labeled. Baby Boomers have grown accustomed to being called such, but many may not like it. And there are plenty of Generation Xers who really don't like that term. So be aware of generational difference, but go easy on the labels!

● ●

SUMMARY

Different generations develop different learning styles and habits. The learning styles and habits of the emerging generations have been strongly affected by their use of technology. Younger learners' comfort with all-things-e, especially computers and the Internet, and their early, intense playing of video games, along with other factors, have made them respond better to training given at a quicker pace, containing a high level of interaction, and providing choices and options.

Boomers, on the other hand, tend to train at a more leisurely pace, use more telling, text-oriented methods, and take a very linear approach to things. Boomers need to modify their habits and add more interaction and choice to the design and delivery of training. How much change and modification depends on the generational composition of the class. In classes with a mix of generations, a variety of techniques and approaches will be necessary, along with the flexibility and willingness to adapt design and delivery when needed.

Pick Up the Pace
to Hold Attention

Ñ ot long ago I attended an Elvis Costello concert with my Generation X daughter. At some point during the concert, the audience became so engaged with the music that they began to stand and jump. I stood along with them and found myself struggling to get into the rhythm of things. I just couldn't find the right beat. Finally I realized that, while I was trying to swing and sway, they were jumping up and down at a constant, driving, incessant pace.

That image of myself trying to swing and sway while all around me younger people are jumping up and down makes a nice analogy for some of the training struggles I've both encountered and observed in the past few years. Most training delivered by a Baby Boomer moves at a leisurely pace, punctuated here and there with a burst of energy, an involving activity, a small-group discussion. If one were to describe the basic tempo or rhythm of the average Boomer style of training, it would be a slow, measured beat of quarter notes: one, two, three, four. The younger generations, however, have grown up to a different beat—a faster, more driving, unrelenting beat—an MTV beat, a twitch-speed melody of sixteenth notes.

Think for a moment about your own style of training. What is the pace or tempo of your training? At what speed do you move through the material? Consider a typical one-day training class and the tempo at which you deliver the material. Maybe you use an energetic, but evenly paced, tempo. Perhaps your approach is very sequential, linear, and rather slow-paced. These slower tempos and teaching paces may be very reassuring to older participants, but they seem frustratingly slow and unnecessary to younger participants.

If you have mostly older participants, you may want to make just a few adjustments to the speed of your training. But if you have a majority of trainees under thirty, you will probably want to pick up the pace and keep things moving fairly quickly throughout your training. This will help you keep their attention and pull them into your content. You can pick up your pace by doing such things as starting your program with a bang, keeping it lively, tightening group activity times, presenting information in less linear fashion, and moving from the use of audiovisual to the use of multimedia.

● ●

START WITH A BANG!

Begin your program with a bang! Members of the younger generations are quite accustomed to having special events begin with an overwhelming or extremely involving event. Most Hollywood action films start in the midst of some catastrophic incident, and it's not until the horrendous possible event has been averted that the opening credits begin. When you begin a video game, you are immediately thrown into an active situation. You must move ahead, make decisions, try various options, learn new skills, deal with failure, and discover pathways, and that's just the first few minutes.

When I talked with younger learners about how to begin a training program, they expressed concern about how long they have to wait before anything happens. They would consistently advise me to "do something right away, something exciting that illustrates the point." How long is it before "anything really happens" in your training programs?

Consider using an especially dynamic type of beginning in programs that contain a large number of younger learners. By immediately beginning with a lively, involving activity, you have a better chance of "hooking" the younger learners; although your other participants may be a little surprised at first, they're going to get hooked too!

● ●

IMMEDIATELY DO SOMETHING DYNAMIC

Not only should the class start with a bang, it should start on time. If the class is scheduled to begin at 9:00 A.M., then at 9:01, begin the opening activity. Do something immediately. Don't stand and talk for the first few minutes. Don't go over class goals and the agenda. Cover those later. Start the class with an involving activity. If possible, make it an experiential learning activity that illustrates a key learning point in a physical way—have them experience the problem, the issue, the situation first-hand. But begin the activity immediately. People who arrive late can join in as they arrive.

And whatever your opening activity, make it challenging! Don't begin with an easy task or a simple introductory or get-acquainted activity. Make the first activity a dynamic one—something that takes energy, needs physical activity, and/or presents a mental challenge. Make it a WOW!

Not too long ago I was giving a two-hour presentation on using training games to a university education class at Northern Illinois University. I had a six-foot by eight-foot electronic rug set up in the front of the room that I was going to use for an activity on reacting to change, but I first distributed a four-page handout and began going over definitions and uses of games and structured activities. Midway through my standard mini-lecture, I took a good look at my Generation X audience. Eyes glazed over, mouths hanging open, bodies slumped in uncomfortable chairs, they were dropping like flies.

I quickly came to my senses, clapped my hands, and ordered everybody to come up front and gather around the carpet. I swiftly explained the rules and regulations and got them trying to cross the carpet without setting off a beep. They were instantly energized, interested, and involved—and remained so well beyond the activity. And that's one of the greatest side benefits of using a really good opening activity—that interest and energy last a long time.

● ●

FOUR WAYS TO START WITH A BANG!

1. Start with Round One.   Have an ongoing contest or activity that continues throughout the day, but hold round one immediately. It doesn't need to be highly competitive, but it should be highly involving and challenging. For example, in a training program where the learning of a physical skill is involved (such as constructing a special sandwich or giving CPR), participants can attempt to demonstrate the skill, following guidelines and within a set amount of time, at various times throughout the program.

2. Start with a "Sound and Light" Show. Have a five-minute multi-media event that poses a question or presents a puzzle that is tied into the topic of the program and in which the group must physically participate in some way. For example, the multi-media event could include a slogan that the audience provides on cue.

3. Start with a Contest. Quickly divide the group into three or four teams and have them compete in some way—folding and flying paper airplanes that go a certain distance, finding items presented on a treasure hunt list, building a house of cards. The activity must be related to the content of the training, either directly or through analogy.

4. Start with a Test. Give a quiz or a true-false test that they take in small groups or with partners. Make the test fun by putting in funny "distracter" items and a few absurd, but true, items. But don't make it easy—make it difficult. Keep the activity moving quickly and have incentives included (being the first finished, having the most right answers, and so forth).

● ●

MAKE IT SNAPPY

Keeping training presentations fairly lively will help keep the interest and attention of younger learners. Answering a question about pace of training, a twenty-six-year-old grad student who had just returned to school after a few years in corporate America complained about the slow pace of training that he had attended: "It was just so slow and so boring that there was no blood going into my brain and I felt like I was about to pass out."

How to Make It Snappy!

Try to Use a Faster Rate. Nothing excessive or extreme, just pick up the pace when presenting your material.

Keep Your "Telling Time" Short. Keep the amount of time you lecture to an absolute minimum. Quickly present a concept, and then have the participants do something with it—discuss it, apply it, critique it, reword it, draw it, chart it, whatever.

Move About the Room More.   Try not to stand in any one place for more than a minute or two. You don't have to exaggerate your moving about or draw attention to your movements, but do move! Whether you are speaking or they are speaking, whether there is an activity occurring or an exercise being carried out, do not stay in any one location for very long.

Use Rhetorical Questions.   You can also punch up your presentation with rhetorical questions. Ask participants a rhetorical question in a slightly louder voice, then pause, move, and continue talking.

Get Them Up and Moving Often.   Set a snappy pace for the participants also. Never let them sit for more than half an hour. Fifteen minutes is even better.

Use the following checklist to pick up the pace of group activities.

EXHIBIT 3.1.   Checklist for Tightening Group Activity Time

_____ Give less time than you normally do for each activity. Shorten time allotments by 10 to 20 percent.

_____ Tell participants exactly how much time they have to do exactly what. Rather than saying things like, "Take the next twenty or thirty minutes and brainstorm ways to address the problem," try being more time exact: "Take the next twenty minutes and brainstorm at least thirty ways to address the problem. OK?" Glance at your watch, then look up: "Twenty minutes, thirty ways, go!"

_____ When work groups report on their activities, give them an exact time limit and stick to it. Explain that there just isn't time to hear everything a group would like to share, so share only the most important information.

_____ Use a clock, a stopwatch, or a timer. Put the clock or timer where it can be seen and/or heard by those reporting.

_____ Agree on a one-minute warning sign and use it. Sit at the back of the room and signal when there is a minute to go.

_____ Get out the gong again. For a bit of fun, and as an extra energizer, use a gong. When a presenter goes over the time allotted, have someone ring the gong. It can really perk things up and establish a lively pace.

Picking the right music can be difficult. You don't want to burden young participants with your generational favorites and you don't want to choose music you *think* they will like. Nor do you want to run into legal issues of playing music without legitimate rights to do so. So have an array of copyright-free music available and try different pieces.

IDEAS FOR USING MUSIC AND SOUND

- Play some lively, fast-paced music in the background as participants work in groups or carry out class activities.

- Let them choose their music. Ask participants what they like. Explain the copyright issues, then let them choose from the available music.

- Elect a class DJ for the day. Have the participants choose a class member to play the music.

- Set a timer to go off every twenty minutes. When the timer goes off, you must change the activity or change some aspect of the activity (get a new partner) or at least have participants stand and stretch.

- Use a gong! Hang a small gong somewhere in the classroom and let the group decide how to use it to keep things lively and moving along.

Present Information Differently

Have Basic Information Posted.   Indicate where information is located around the learning environment, but don't read it to the participants. For example, have the class purpose and goals posted somewhere easily seen where they can be referred to as needed. Do the same with housekeeping information such as break and lunch times, location of restrooms, smoking policy, and so on.

Have Key Concepts in View at All Times.   Use bright, colorful posters hanging on the wall to present basic, key information. Arrange the information in short segments with interesting graphics.

Present Information in Chunks.   Do not slowly present information in a series of overheads or in a sequence of dissolving slides. If there are ten characteristics, show all ten at once.

Have Extra Information Available for Taking.   Consider having a flyer with information about yourself available on a side table near the door. You can introduce yourself and give two or three bits of key information, then walk over and show the participants the flyers by the door. You can also set out articles, bibliographies, and other types of information on the training topic for anyone who is interested.

Use Pocket Folders.   Instead of a workbook, a participant guide, or ADTRB (another damn three-ring binder), distribute pocket folders. Have various materials available around the room and let participants gather the information they want. Have computers and printers available with class material on them. Participants can print out whatever materials they want. They can also type up and print out class notes, group reports, and flip chart information should they want it.

Have All Information Available on Computer Disks.   Anyone who wants a disk can have one.

● ●

LEAVE THE READING TO THE PARTICIPANTS

As one younger learner told me when I asked about annoying habits of some older trainers: "The worst instructors are those who have no movement. They just stand there and drone on."

You can pick up the pace of your program and keep the attention of participants by not reading to them. Do not stand in front of overheads or posters and read their contents aloud. Walk briskly to the poster or stand to the side of the overhead or slide and say something like, "What do you think of this? Does it make sense?" Pause and let them read and comment, then walk on to something else.

If you can't break yourself of the habit of reading posted material out loud to the class, consider appointing a "No Reading Monitor." Give him or her a squeeze horn and if you goof and start reading material out loud to the class, the monitor can honk away.

FROM AV TO MULTIMEDIA

When Generation Xers use the term multimedia, they don't mean audiotapes, videos, and overhead transparencies. They mean short segments of video taken from movies and television programs, downloaded video clips and movie trailers from the Internet, and music samples from CDs. When was the last time you showed a video clip? How many movie trailers have you watched on the Internet? Learn how to use multimedia and use it often.

Four Ways to Add More Multimedia

1. Show a movie clip that illustrates a key point that you are making.
You can take it from a video or DVD, or sometimes they can be downloaded from the web.

2. Show pictures and various images that demonstrate your point or illustrate your subject matter. You can download these from the web and project them on the screen.

3. Show short segments of video games as examples of concepts. For instance, as an example of frustration and persistence show a clip from *Harry Potter and the Chamber of Secrets* where Harry is "de-gnoming" the garden by tossing out all of the garden gnomes!

4. Show digital pictures or video segments from real life. Use these as samples of what exists or how things are. For example, instead of talking about common customer complaints, videotape a few customers at the complaint desk and show that!

If You Must Use Traditional AV. . .

Use Ten-Second Overheads. If you show an overhead, do not leave it up for more than ten seconds. If more time is required to discuss what is written on the overhead, consider having a chart posted with the same information.

Use Electronic Slides Sparingly. Keep electronic slides to a minimum. Consider using a short series of slides with no words, only graphics, to make a few key points.

Make Videos More Interactive.   Keep video time to a minimum. If you must use a video that is more than five minutes long, stand near the screen and periodically stop the video and ask questions.

Encourage Learners to Talk Back to Videos.   Ask your learners to become verbally involved with the video—not with funny, sarcastic comments, but any comments that are pertinent to the content. They can set up their own guidelines for how to do this. They can take turns using the remote control.

Let Learners Interrupt Videos.   When they want to interrupt, they can call out, "Stop" or raise their hands, and you can press the pause button. I do this with an "aging" career development video that makes many good points, but is a bit outdated. The participants are always hesitant at first, but it doesn't take long for them to get into it. I sit in the middle of the room and back a bit and hit the pause button when a hand goes up. The twenty-five-minute video ends up taking forty-five minutes, but we have excellent discussion along the way.

● ●

SUMMARY

To sum things up, let me reiterate that keeping learners of all ages interested and tuned in to the training is important in all training situations. Maintaining a lively pace is particularly important to younger learners. Check the design and delivery of your programs to make sure you start things with a bang and keep your delivery snappy. Consider using music, sound, and multimedia to give an energetic tempo to your training. Look for ways to present information that do not slow down the overall pace of the program.

Increase Interaction to Engage Learners

Interactivity is of the essence. Younger learners crave interaction—with each other, with the material, with problems and information, with experts and people who really know. They don't want to be told; they want to find out. This is the one factor that always comes out at the top of the list when members of the younger generation describe an ideal learning situation. As one university graduate student explained to me, "The ideal seminar would involve a variety of activities and move at a fairly rapid pace. Show us the concept and then give us an activity to apply it, either individually or as a group."

Many of today's younger learners were educated in classrooms where they were guided and encouraged to "find out for themselves." Discovery learning, engaged learning, and other such approaches that have been popular in American schools over the last two decades focus young learners on what they want to know and how to find out. Discovering answers and obtaining information on their own is something they have come to expect in a learning situation. Giving them a handout of the Top Ten Customer Complaints, for example, may not be nearly as effective as letting them sort through a hundred customer complaint forms and discover the top ten complaints for themselves.

As was mentioned in Chapter Two, getting learners involved is so important that you want to do it immediately in your training programs. Consider having games such as board games, card games, construction games, and so forth ready for participants to begin using as soon as they arrive. Or have paper-and-pencil puzzles available on the subject matter and let them start solving the puzzles as soon as they come in. Give points or tokens or small prizes for every puzzle they solve! Other ways to increase interaction include telling less and letting them do more, providing for discovery, and allowing for risk taking and failure.

FOUR SHORT, EASY INTERACTIONS

1. Pose a question and ask participants to turn to a neighbor and discuss the possible answer.

2. Quickly number the participants one through four, five, or six and ask all people with the same number to find each other and form a small group to discuss a question you give them or to share something that they have been working on individually, such as an assessment or quiz.

3. Number the participants in such a way that there are only two people in the room with the same numbers. For example, in a class of twenty people have them number off one through ten and then repeat the process. Ask the two number ones to get together, the two number twos, the two threes, and so on. Give them five minutes to share and compare their results on an assessment or their answers to a quiz.

4. Ask the participants to find a partner they have not had the opportunity to talk with yet that day.

• •

USE GAMES AND ACTIVITIES TO INCREASE INTERACTION

Most learners in general, and young learners in particular, prefer an active approach to learning. Physical action games and simulation games that are fast-paced and require players to literally move a great deal as they discover how a particular activity is done can be very motivating to learners of all ages. When I asked a focus group I was working with how much of training should be fun and games, someone called out, "Half and half. Half fun and half games!" They were joking, yes, but they were also serious.

And there's more to playing training games than increasing interaction. With a well-designed and delivered training game, you can reinforce key learning concepts, provide for the safe practice of new skills, and supply an arena for discussion and assimilation of new information—all in a stimulating, interactive context. The following list presents eight types of games that increase interaction and engage learners.

Eight Types of Involving Games

1. Board Games.   Design and use board games on your topic. These can include question-and-answer cards that players draw, answer, and then move around the board according to a point system. Board games can also be designed to give participants more and more information on a topic, allowing them to eventually solve a problem or answer a key question. Structure the games so that they are fast-paced. (For an example, see Game 19, Across the Board, in Part Two of this book.)

2. Card Games.   Design card games that use specially constructed decks of cards that contain subject matter from the training. Games can involve manipulating the cards in some way, such as sorting or rank ordering them or answering questions related to the content of the cards. (For examples, see Game 10, Find the Top Ten, and Game 8, Two Card Audit, in Part Two of this book.)

3. Matrix Games.   Provide challenging matrix games. Matrix games are paper-and-pencil games that require participants to cover boxes on a matrix by demonstrating a specific skill or knowledge or to fill in the boxes with particular information. As participants get all right answers in a row or column, or diagonally across their matrix cards, they receive a prize. Make these games fast-moving. (See Game 14, Generational Bingo, in Part Two of this book.)

4. Construction Games.   Devise construction games for a literal hands-on activity. These games require players to build a three-dimensional object of some sort using various materials such as interlocking building toys, modeling clay, construction paper, pipe cleaners, and so forth. (As an example, see Game 1, Sculpt Away, in Part Two of this book.)

5. Paper-and-Pencil Puzzles.   Use paper-and-pencil puzzles, quizzes, and assessments on the topic to get participants involved in gathering information to solve problems. (See Game 4, A Matter of Definition, in Part Two of this book.)

6. Physical Puzzles.   Prepare jigsaw puzzles on the topic for individuals or small groups to solve. Give points, tokens, or prizes for puzzles solved. (For an example of a physical puzzle game using tangram puzzles, see Game 11, The Whole Is Greater, in Part Two of this book.)

7. Wall Games.   Use copies of puzzles, word games, quizzes, crossword puzzles, and such posted on the walls for small groups to solve. Since players must go to the game and stand as they play, this also becomes a good way to get people up and moving around. (For a sample of this type of game, see Game 2, Word Search Mania, in Part Two of this book.)

8. Flip-Chart Games.   Design flip-chart games that call for small groups of people to stand or sit around a flip chart. There can be some type of puzzle or quiz on the flip chart that they must solve or they might use the flip chart to record their ideas as they try to solve a problem. Short flip-chart games and activities are another easy way to get learners up and about and doing something. (See Game 17, Ready, Set, Goal, in Part Two of this book.)

the nitty gritty

Ideas for Small Prizes

- FOOD—popcorn, peanuts, sunflower seeds, wrapped hard candy, small packs of popular candy, fruit, small packs of chips, pretzels, and so forth.

- ITEMS—funny pencils and erasers, big brightly colored plastic paper clips, funny magnets, funny Post-it® Notes, Gumby® and Pokey®, Slinkys®, Silly Putty®, squeeze toys, stickers, balloons, Koosh® balls, poppers, or fake money.

DON'T SHOW AND TELL

The Boomer propensity to tell is probably the biggest turnoff to younger learners. The quickest way to lose a young audience is to lecture to them. As one learner from the emerging generations told me, "I dislike long lectures with no interaction of students. It gets hard to concentrate when a person just continuously babbles on."

Four Ways to Tell Less and Let Them Do More

1. Cut Way Back on Lecturing.   The quickest way to lose a young audience is to lecture to them. Any time you find yourself talking for more than ten minutes, look for another way to present what you are talking about.

2. Ask and Let Them Find.   Pose a question or a concern, or present a topic or an issue; then provide access to information, including electronic access, and let the participants discover what's what. Have them report their results in an involving way, such as constructing posters that participants can walk around and view or giving five-minute "newscasts" reporting their findings.

3. Make Raw Data or Assimilated Information Available.   Let participants analyze and discover underlying themes, trends, and so forth and then make recommendations.

4. Let Them Do the Work.   Your job is to guide, facilitate, motivate.

● ●

TRY MORE COMFORT AND LESS COMPETITION

Baby Boomer culture is basically competitive. There were so many of us as we were growing up that we fell almost naturally into a competitive stance toward most situations. We competed for our parents' attention with our 3.4 brothers and sisters. We competed for our teacher's attention in our crowded classrooms. We competed for scholarships, dorm rooms, and part-time jobs, and then we moved on to competing for real jobs, promotions, and attention from the boss. Many of us are still competing as to who can look younger than he or she really is!

The emerging generations are somewhat less competitive in their approach to things. They had fewer brothers and sisters growing up and were more involved in teamwork and group projects in their school years. That's not to say there are no competitive individuals among the younger generations. They are still competitive, of course, but their general approach to the world of work and to the world of learning is not an immediately competitive one. They are more accustomed to working cooperatively in small groups to achieve the goal.

● ●

ALLOW MORE PRUDENT RISK TAKING

Connected to their less-competitive nature is the younger person's attitude toward risk and failure. In general, younger people are less risk-averse in learning situations than are their Boomer elders. No one wins a video game without taking risks and learning from numerous failures. As young electronic game players, these people shared their mistakes and learned from each other's mistakes.

With the above in mind, design games and activities that require participants to take risks and sometimes fail. Be sure to include discussion and debriefing activities that explore risk taking and dealing with failure beforehand and sometimes during and after the game or activity. Find ways to give credit or points for trying and testing, and encourage collaboration where participants can share what they learn from failure and work together to solve problems.

However, if there is a mixture of generations in the group, or if "the boss" is in the room, it would be prudent to be careful with too much risk taking. No one likes to make mistakes or appear to be too much of a risk taker in front of the boss. In general, many older workers are not comfortable making too many mistakes and taking too many risks. Sound like walking on eggshells? Hey, you're a pro.

● ●

PROVIDE FOR DISCOVERY

One of the joys of electronic game playing is discovery. Discovering a new path, a new weapon, a secret tunnel, or a new technique enables you to be a better player and achieve the goal sooner. The same joy of discovery can be taken advantage of in the classroom. One young woman I interviewed described a good seminar as follows: "A good seminar would be fast-paced, with a lot of chances to apply what we're learning and discover things ourselves."

 ## Four Ways to Provide Discovery in Your Training

1. Design with Discovery in Mind.   Create activities in which participants gather clues (data, information) that can eventually be analyzed and used to achieve a goal. Design interactions that allow for the analyzing of information and the drawing of conclusions. Have learners share their findings and conclusions. (See Game 8, Two-Card Audit, for an example of this.)

2. Use Resources.   Consider having a classroom resource table that participants can visit throughout the class. Perhaps have copies of a few articles that they can take and a few books that they can browse through. Have a couple of newspapers that they can read and a computer that they can use to go online to find information. Offer rewards for reviews and opinion statements on what they read. Have paper and felt pens on the resource table for them to write reviews and post them on the wall.

3. Assign Tasks.   Having participants complete some type of task related to the topic is a good way to involve them in the learning and lead them into discovery. You can ask them to use various materials and build a representation of a key concept or use a building activity as a way to experience a program topic such as team building. Make the activity fast-paced by giving a time limit, setting rules or conditions, and offering a prize. A skilled debriefing of any activity can be an occasion for discovery. (See Game 18, Involve to Solve, in Part Two of this book.)

4. Try a Sorting Activity.   A sorting activity can also be very involving. Have a variety of items that need to be sorted according to a theory or process being studied in the training. Consider using cards with different examples of whatever is being studied and asking participants to sort the cards into categories. You can also have participants rank-order a number of items according to various criteria, perhaps ranging from "most important" to "least important." Keep things exciting by having a time limit. (For an example of this, see Game 10, Find the Top Ten, in Part Two of this book.)

● ●

SUMMARY

Interactivity is extremely important when dealing with learners from Generation X and the Millennial generation. Malcolm Knowles, the great scholar-practitioner of adult learning, in his book *The Adult Learner* (1998), described, among other characteristics, adult learners as autonomous and self-directed. He argued that adults don't want to be lectured at and inundated with data. They want to be actively involved in their own learning. Today's younger adult learners would heartily agree with him.

To engage these young adult learners and, for that matter, learners of all ages, it is imperative that you increase your use of interactive games and activities. Lecture less and let them do more. Provide opportunities for learners to discover things for themselves. The more involved they are, the more they will learn.

Link to the Learner to Make It Meaningful

If you've been teaching or training for a number of years, you probably have a good feel for your material and your audiences. You've learned what works and what doesn't. You've come up with some especially good examples and illustrations. It can feel so good when you're on a roll. You're standing up there explaining something and you see the light bulbs go off. You make a comparison, you give an example, and the participants laugh, they nod, they get it!

Then comes the day when you notice that a number of people are not laughing or nodding. They may be sitting politely waiting for you to continue or, good grief, they may be rolling their eyes and grimacing! What's wrong with these people? Your clever analogy to Sgt. Pepper, the pun on the famous Beach Boys song, completely miss the target! Whoosh, over their heads and out the door. And there you stand.

The third need that Emerging Generation learners express regarding Boomer trainers is the need for relevancy. If younger learners think that we Boomers know little, if anything, about them and their lives, then we lose credibility. If they perceive us to be aware of their "culture" and able to relate to some of the issues and circumstances of their lives, they become more open and receptive to the content of our training.

Learning about the culture of the younger generations is important. So is including some of their cultural norms in our training programs, such as using technology, including a variety of hands-on activities, and stimulating their senses as they learn.

● ●

LEARN ABOUT EMERGING GENERATION CULTURE

This is how one Generation X learner explained to me his inability to connect with the instructor in a recent "new employee" workshop that he had attended: "The instructor—she's middle-aged, she has a family, she hasn't been to a bar or a club in ten years. My life and hers have no common bounds."

This was a twenty-five-year-old talking about a thirty-eight-year-old. Think what his comments might have been about a fifty-year-old! It is imperative that Boomer trainers get to know more about the cultures of younger learners. Not to act falsely hip, but to make appropriate references, to give pertinent examples, and to base information in a relevant context. And while visiting a Generation X club or bar might not be the answer to linking to your younger learners, it might not hurt. Visiting a favorite Generation X club might be a real mind-expanding experience. Watching a few hours of MTV might also do the trick!

You can learn about the culture of the younger generations much like you would learn about any other culture: read about the culture, talk with people from that culture, and visit the culture. Speak with young people. Ask them about themselves and their friends and what they like to do. Then listen. And be sure that you really listen. A perceptive thirty-year-old graduate student explained to me, "There is an exchange of energy when you talk with someone. You can tell who is actually interested in hearing what you are saying."

How to Become Familiar with Emerging Generation Cultures

GENERATION X CULTURE (AGES 27 TO 39)

- Watch some reality TV shows such as "Survivor" and MTV's "Real World" and "Road Rules." Or check out "Buffy the Vampire Slayer."

- Read a few articles on salon.com.

- Read any or all of the three-book trilogy *Lord of the Rings.* Or watch a *Lord of the Rings* movie such as *The Fellowship of the Ring* or *The Two Towers.* Watch *Star Wars* again.

- Read a few Generation X magazines such as *Spin, Wired,* and *Fast Company.*

- Read a couple of Nick Hornsby novels, such as *High Fidelity* or *About a Boy,* or watch the movies that were made from them.

- Play Tetris®, Mario Brothers®, and Mortal Kombat®, then move on to Myst®, Zelda®, and Grand Theft Auto®.

- If you have never watched "The Simpsons," do so! Check out "South Park" while you're at it. If you can find "Beavis and Butthead," watch a couple of episodes.

- Try sipping a mocha cappuccino while nibbling on a scone or some biscotti.

NET GENERATION CULTURE (AGES 10 TO 26)

- Read the Harry Potter books. Read a few Goosebumps books and a Lemony Snicket book or two.

- Visit theForce.net or onering.net. Visit cheatcc.com or gameFAQ.com for guides to popular games. See emode.com for personality tests. For younger Next-Gen culture, visit nick.com and cartoonnetwork.com.

- Play some video games such as Final Fantasy® or any of the four Grand Theft Auto® games, or try an online role-playing game like Diablo2®.

- If you don't know what a Rugrat is, find out.

- Watch TV programs like "Will and Grace," "The Gilmore Girls," "Everwood," or, for younger members of this generation, watch "Blues Clues" and "SpongeBob SquarePants."

- Try a Mountain Dew Live Wire and snack on a few poppers.

DO A CULTURAL AUDIT OF YOUR MATERIALS

● Check your notes and outlines. See if you can find examples that you routinely use that refer to events or popular culture prior to the nineties. Add newer examples and use both, or choose what to use according to each audience that comes your way.

● Do a similar audit of your printed materials. Check all workbooks and handouts for outdated information, ideas, and examples. Whenever possible include a variety of information and examples that would appeal to a variety of generations. And don't forget to check your bibliographies. It's all right to have a few "classic" works cited, but the majority of your references should be quite recent.

● Consider hiring a "younger-generation auditor." Get someone from the younger, emerging generations to go through your materials and perhaps sit in on a class or two. Ask your auditor to give you feedback. Get his or her ideas and suggestions for increasing your younger-generation cultural knowledge and follow his or her advice!

● ●

CHARACTERISTICS OF THE IDEAL INSTRUCTOR

One of the items on a questionnaire that I used with seventy younger learners between the ages of nineteen and thirty-nine asked for the qualities or characteristics of the "ideal" instructor. It was heartening to see that the qualities they most admired were not so different from what learners of all ages look for. Here are some characteristics they used to describe the ideal instructor:

● Energetic and down-to-earth; enthusiastic, intelligent

● Knows a lot about the subject being presented

● Is passionate about it

● Good sense of humor, funny, entertaining

● Does not intimidate people

● Able to include everyone in the conversation

● Cares about students on an individual basis

- Listens as well as lectures

- Good at making the audience feel comfortable

- Upbeat, approachable, but not overwhelming

So if you are all of these things, plus you have a good feel for the culture and life situations of your audience, you are well on your way to linking to younger learners.

● ●

MAKE USE OF TECHNOLOGY IN YOUR TRAINING

Technology is extremely helpful in engaging younger learners. It is a natural part of their lives. Incorporating the use of computers, the Internet, and e-mail into your training is the bare minimum required. Try going above and beyond these basics by doing some of the following:

- Use multimedia in your presentations. Show film and television clips. Play music that illustrates concepts and ideas that you are discussing. Have the participants use technology in their activities.

- Use a digital camera during your programs. Take pictures of groups discussing, participants working, and projects being presented. Display the pictures or video during debriefings and summaries. Make digital pictures available after class on your website.

- Have your portable computer with you for all training events, plugged in, connected to the Internet, and ready to go. Encourage students to bring their laptops to class or have computers in the classroom that students can use throughout the training as needed.

● ●

ASK FOR HELP WHEN YOU NEED IT

It is interesting to talk with younger learners about the technology fears and inadequacies of some Boomer trainers. They often do not seem as concerned with the fact that our use of technology is lacking as they do with the fact that we do not make greater efforts to learn. Their view is that we should just explore, make mistakes, and mess around with something until we learn how to do it. Of course, we could turn and ask someone how to do whatever it is that we want to do. This is the younger learners' way of learning about new technologies. A young woman in her late twenties advised me, "Be open to the fact that your students might know more than you and that's OK because we can mutually learn from each other."

A FEW WAYS THAT YOU CAN ASK FOR HELP

- Ask for information and demonstrations when you see students using technology that is unfamiliar to you or when you hear them talking about technology that you do not understand. A great way to link with your learners is to be a learner yourself and let them teach you!

- Have a few "digital consultants" that you can go to with questions and concerns. Get their ideas and input as to how to maximize the use of technology in your training.

- Don't pretend to know when you don't really know. The worst thing that you can do when it comes to digital ineptness or linking to the younger generations is to pretend to know more than you do. Learn as much as you can, but don't fake it. To quote a sharp young woman in a focus group I held, "I just want to say [to Boomer Generation trainers], avoid faux hip-ness. There is nothing more embarrassing for someone my age."

● ●

STIMULATE THE SENSES OF YOUR LEARNERS

While Boomer learning has more or less been dominated by text, the younger generations of learners have taken in as much of their learning from graphics, sound, and physical manipulation as they have from text. To progress in a video game, you must coordinate the movements of your hands and thumbs with the changing visual images on the screen and respond to a variety of changing audio cues. A learning environment that offers little in the way of graphics and sound and requires almost no tactile participation stands the chance of boring young people, even if those young people are interested in the subject matter and want to learn. As a young woman of twenty-five explained while discussing workshops she had attended, "I want a lot of hands-on in a workshop. The more I can work with what I'm learning, the more I'll take with me and remember afterward."

For many years now, proponents of accelerated learning have extolled the benefits of appealing to all of the senses in learning situations. What this means to learning is that different individuals will respond to different stimuli. And many Boomer trainers subscribe to the excellent principles of accelerated and "brain-friendly" learning. But bringing the senses into the classroom is not always an easy thing to do. And offering graphics and sound that come anywhere near the quality that video-hypnotized learners are accustomed to is almost impossible.

The ideal situation may be to produce digital-game-based learning events, as Mark Prensky purports in his book *Digital Game-Based Learning,* but the costs of producing such games is prohibitive to many; until it becomes less so, other approaches are needed to bring more graphics, sound, options, and interactivity into the classroom. The challenge is to do so in ways that engage all learners without coming across as unprofessional and tacky. So how do you do that? The following lists make some good suggestions!

USE MORE VISUALS AND GRAPHICS

- Pair icons or simple visual images with your key concepts and use them thoughout the training in all of your training materials.

- Instead of giving examples in text, give them in pictures. Try to find and use pictures that illustrate your key points. Workbooks, participant guides, and handouts should all contain illustrative and illuminating visual images.

- Display movie posters that illustrate or tie into your training themes.

- Consider using a short series of slides with no words, only graphics, to make a few key points.

INCORPORATE SOUND, AROMA, AND TASTE IN TRAINING

- Make use of music. Play music during group activities. Have an array of copyright-free music available and try different pieces.

- Use sound effects throughout the day. Use a whistle, horn, bell, gong, or similar sound-producing item to call attention, announce the end of activities, or proclaim the end of a break.

- Use buzzers. Have two different buzzers or horns and use them to signal right or wrong answers. Use them in games and activities to determine which individual or group answers first.

● Design games and activities to include noise in some way. Provide each small group with a "noise maker" that is to be used at certain times during the game or activity. Require card decks to be shuffled. Provide game pieces that make noise as they are moved around a game board.

● Use flowers. Have a bouquet of flowers in the classroom. Give learners flowers as prizes.

● Make popcorn as participants are playing a board game and take around bowls of popcorn for them to have as they play.

● Use scented markers for flip charts, name cards, and other activities.

● Do NOT burn incense or candles. Many people have allergies to these.

● Have refreshments available during the program to add taste to the learning environment. Try setting out bowls of mints and hard candies on participant tables. Use various edible prizes throughout your program and throw small pieces of hard candy to people who participate in discussions and/or who make good comments and observations.

Ten Ways to Be More Tactile

1. Keep It Moving.   Use activities where participants mix and mingle and even touch! Ask them to shake hands. Give them something to pass along to one another.

2. Hand Things Out.   Have samples and examples that can be passed around.

3. Involve Them Creatively.   Distribute colored markers at some point and ask for some task to be done on paper using the colored markers.

4. Use Cards.   Provide decks of learning cards with key information, various ideas, or techniques to use written on them and have participants rank-order them or sort them into categories.

5. Play Games.   Try board games where players roll dice and move tokens around the board. Such games can also include decks of Q&A cards, scorekeeping devices, and noise-makers to use for right and wrong answers.

6. Use Physical Activity.   Have construction activities where participants must physically construct something using various materials or building supplies.

7. Use Flip Charts.   Use flip-chart activities that require participants to write on flip charts, tear off flip-chart paper, and tape it to the wall.

8. Bring Out Hats.   Have a variety of hats available that participants can choose to wear for "report outs" and group presentations.

9. Provide Props.   Find items that can be used in various games and activities such as scarves, umbrellas, hats, fake glasses, and similar items.

10. Ask for Help.   Let participants distribute handouts and materials and rearrange the learning environment as needed. Instead of passing out materials yourself, enlist the help of participants to do so. When the room needs to be rearranged, let the learners do it.

● ●

SUMMARY

After years of doing training, linking with an audience of our peers almost comes naturally, but connecting with an ever-changing audience of people younger than we are takes an ongoing effort on our part. To maintain our credibility and enhance the relevancy of our content, we must understand our younger audience and illustrate our material in ways that are meaningful to them and their lives. And that means increasing our comfort levels with technology and using technology in our training. It also means including a variety of hands-on activities and stimulating participants' senses as they learn.

Offer Options
for Nonlinear Learning

Have you ever watched a twenty-something work or study? There is nothing linear about it. There may be a book or two open, papers here and there, but the computer has two or three screens going at the same time while instant message alerts flash in the corner. Online, twenty-somethings move from site to site, taking in information, saving this, eliminating that. The younger generations live much of their lives this way—connected electronically and interacting simultaneously in a variety of media. Doing things one at a time, in sequential order, in a step-by-step fashion is not only boring to younger learners, but it is downright difficult.

Malcolm Knowles (1998) described adult learners as autonomous and self-directed. This is especially true of the younger adults among us. We Boomer trainers must rethink and re-design our approach to training to include more options, a variety of parallel processes, and random access to an assortment of learning alternatives. Let the learners choose the how of getting to the endpoint, or at least offer them a variety of pathways that may be taken.

● ●

GIVE THE LEARNERS MORE CHOICES

Design training situations where learners make choices, big choices and small choices. Look at your tried-and-true exercises and activities. Find ways to make them less linear and more open to a variety of options.

For years in an Anticipating the Future class I taught, I would drag recent books, magazines, and articles to class and assign small groups to research issues that affected their future and then make presentations. Over time, I noticed two things. First, the younger participants were not as comfortable going through the material as the older participants, and second, I was more and more printing out information that I had found on the Internet and adding it to my books and magazines. When I changed the activity to include "finding your own information, online or wherever," the younger learners perked up and went off and found their own information. This broadened the scope of information that was included, and it enhanced their credibility and ownership of the results. I also saw my role changing from the telling teacher to the guiding facilitator.

TEN WAYS TO ADD CHOICE TO YOUR TRAINING

1. Give learners the choice of doing an activity on their own or in a group.

2. Let learners decide which of two, or three, or more activities they will do.

3. Offer class material in printed form, on a CD, or accessible online.

4. Don't assign seats. Let participants choose where they want to sit.

5. Let small groups of learners decide the form and style of group presentations—stand-up, audio, video, slides, posters, or whatever.

6. Design game boards that have different routes that can be taken to reach the finish line.

7. For board games, have a variety of different and unique tokens from which players can choose.

8. Use card-sorting activities where participants can rank-order items or choose which items are most important to them.

9. Design physical action games and simulation games that are fast-paced and require players to choose from a variety of options often.

10. Have a very engrossing small-group activity right before lunch. Make it impossible to finish the activity by the appointed lunchtime. When the lunch hour approaches, tell the groups that they need to have their projects finished by the time class begins again at 1 P.M. and that they may take their lunch break any time they like.

DESIGN GAMES THAT OFFER CHOICES

- Design game boards that have different routes that can be taken to reach the finish line.

- Have a variety of different and unique tokens from which players can choose when they play board games.

- Use card-sorting activities where participants can rank-order items or choose which items are most important to them. (See Game 10, Find the Top Ten, in Part Two of this book.)

- Design action games and simulation games that require players to choose from a variety of options. (See Game 18, Involve to Solve, in Part Two of this book.)

the nitty gritty

Where to Find Small, Unique Items to Use as Tokens

- Teacher supply stores

- Craft and hobby stores

- Hardware and home improvement stores

- Sewing and fabric stores

- Toy departments everywhere

DESIGN FOR RANDOM ACCESS AND SIMULTANEOUS OPTIONS

Many standard training programs have a linear overall design structure. All participants begin at the same place, go through the same activities at the same time, and end together at the same time and place. The design and set-up of the learning environment accommodates this linear approach: the trainer at the front of the class and the participants at tables and chairs lined up or in a U-shape facing the trainer at the front.

Other program and learning environment designs are possible, designs that would provide for a nonlinear, simultaneous options approach. Create a learning environment where the participants sit in groups of four to six around small, round tables. Design learning corners or learning pods around the room.

One Generation X graduate student in telecommunications that I spoke with had just returned from a seminar and was very impressed with the flexible, open design of the program. Evidently the same content was presented in a variety of formats and participants could choose what they wanted to attend. "It was nice," he explained, "because there were different types of speakers—motivational types, laid-back types, discussion leader types, and so forth. When I talked to people afterward, everyone had pretty much learned the same thing, but the different presentation styles were there and you could choose on your own."

While we might not always be able to design for large, simultaneous events and options, there are ways to design simultaneous options into our standard training programs. The following list gives you some ideas of how to do that.

Put Some Simultaneous Options into Your Programs

Offer Choices. Assign a number of tasks to be completed and a time to reconvene, then let the participants get on with it in their own preferred styles.

Be Flexible. Accept learners doing more than one thing at a time. Do not take offense if participants do not seem to be paying complete attention and work on another task as they listen to you.

Offer an Ongoing Learning Environment. Set up a room that offers continuous learning opportunities and let students come in and out as they have time, need, or whatever.

Use Stand-alones.   Design modules that can be done in any order. Have a mix of modules available—some tutor-led, some classroom-led, some written, some on CD, and so forth. Have all modules available and let learners go back and forth and in and out and pick and choose to meet their needs.

Conduct Simultaneous Events.   Let learners choose which events to attend. Provide learning that is continuous, simultaneous, and learner-controlled. Let the learners learn as much as they want and end the learning when they choose.

Provide Internet Access.   Provide online accessibility before, during, and after any training program.

Use Human Resources.   Offer connections to subject-matter experts and "gurus." Design your training with electronic access to teachers, trainers, mentors, and various subject-matter experts.

• •

CUSTOMIZE THE LEARNING AS YOU GO ALONG

The ability of instructors to be flexible was a trait much admired by the younger learners I interviewed. When asked about the characteristics of ideal instructors, they made comments such as "open-minded, flexible, willing to go against lesson plans from time to time," "willing to adjust to their audience," and "someone willing to change and try new things." One young man put it like this: "An effective instructor can 'read' the participants well and gauge his or her session accordingly. If there are changes that need to be made in the use of media, the delivery, etcetera, an effective instructor can do so."

It's not really difficult to be flexible with an agenda or even to let the needs of your learners dictate the agenda. If we instructors know our material well and have already thought through a number of ways to present that material, then we can be flexible and adaptable to those who are present at any given delivery. A young woman in her late twenties I talked with suggested, "The presenter has to be able to allow the pace to be fluid; have something in mind, but allow for questions and new directions." I like this concept of being fluid. As trainers, we have certain goals to achieve, particular material to be covered, but how we go about doing so does not always have to be the same.

IDEAS FOR CUSTOMIZING THE LEARNING

- Have a variety of illustrations and examples ready so that you can pick and choose those that best fit the audience.

- Use more than one illustration or example for audiences of mixed generations.

- Have two or three learning activities ready for the same learning objective and choose the one that seems to best fit the group. Or let them choose!

- Let the learners determine how much time should be spent on each agenda topic.

- Adjust the type of discussion and activity to group style or subgroup styles. For more active, talkative groups or participants, use large-group discussion and large-group activities. For quieter, more introverted groups or participants, use small-group discussion and small-group activities. For mixed groups, use mixed types of activities.

• •

SUMMARY

Offering options and following a less linear approach to designing and delivering training is probably the most difficult adjustment to make to our Boomer training style. Approaching teaching and training in a straightforward, sequential manner has been so thoroughly ingrained in us, and it seems so natural, especially to those of us who are "J" on the last Myers-Briggs scale. But to engage the emerging generations, to obtain their consideration of our content and objectives, options, choices, random access, and customization must be present in our training design and delivery.

Make It Fun
to Keep Them Learning

IF WE HAVE TIME BEFORE LUNCH, I HAVE A GAME THAT WE CAN TRY.

WHOOPEE!

ANOTHER ONE OF *THOSE* GAMES WHERE WE STAND AROUND IN A CIRCLE AND SEE HOW MANY STUPID THINGS WE CAN MAKE OUT OF A TOOTHBRUSH.

What is fun? Fun is a feeling of enjoyment. When learners are caught up in the learning, when they are excited and energized by what they are doing, they have that feeling of enjoyment. Time seems to fly by. This is the same feeling one has playing a really good video game. The pleasure comes from the high level of involvement, the interaction with other players, the competition that's involved, the mastering of skills, and the increasing of your abilities over time. All of these factors work together to make the activity fun.

I remember walking along the sidelines of a training room once while the members of my class sat in small groups playing a board game that I had designed to allow them to practice a model that the class was designed around. They were rolling dice, moving tokens, drawing cards, reading them out loud, and earnestly discussing the answers. As I walked past one table, a young man looked up and, with a knowing nod, he said, "I know what you're doing. You're letting us have fun with this game, but you're really having us practice the model, aren't you?" I pleaded guilty and walked on.

We must engage our learners and keep them learning by infusing our training with learning situations that have high levels of learner involvement, interaction with other learners, and the sense of growing competency. To accomplish this, we can design into our training programs plenty of immediate performance feedback and a variety of incentives. We can include games and activities that are challenging, involving, and interactive and that capture the imagination of our learners. We can incorporate themes and motifs that add fun and enjoyment.

HOW DO YOU KNOW THEY'RE HAVING FUN?

- You hear them laugh.
- You see them smile.
- The noise level increases.
- Participants say things like "cool," "neat," "hey," "yeah," "wow," and "yes!"
- Participants moan and groan when you end the activity.
- Learners beg for more.

Ways to Add Fun

Start with a Bang.   First impressions are lasting impressions. Make your participants glad they showed up by having an opening activity that is challenging, involving, and fun.

Do More.   Decrease the amount of telling and increase the amount of doing. No matter how great a speaker or presenter you are, younger learners prefer hands-on involvement. Again, make that involvement challenging, involving, and fun!

Mix It Up.   Use fast, action-based games and competitive activities. Such games and activities do not have to be long or involved, but they do need to appear throughout the training.

Make It Interesting.   Make the learning environment pleasant and attractive. Put up posters, charts, and inviting visuals. Have flowers and bowls of mints around. Have a resource or reference table with flyers, handouts, articles, and free samples available to take.

Use Lots of Rewards and Incentives.   Include prizes, awards, and special privileges whenever possible.

Enjoy.   Have fun yourself and enjoy what you are doing.

the nitty gritty

Some Possible Props for Training

- Hats of various sorts and sizes

- Fake microphones

- Fake money

- Rubber chickens

- Four-foot thermometers

- Large fake aspirins and Band-Aids®

- Penalty flags

THE ROLE OF FEEDBACK AND INCENTIVES

I remember a lecturer once who told of a real breakthrough in increasing athletes' running times at a state university somewhere. It seems that large electronic time monitors were set out all around the track, thus giving runners continuous feedback. This immediate and constant feedback allowed them to continually improve their performance. This is certainly one of the most engrossing aspects of computer games. You are continually receiving positive or negative reinforcement of your behaviors.

Incentives also keep the video game player playing. Take the concept of earning extra lives in video games as an example. You can play the game as long as you are alive on the screen; in fact, in most games, you start out with more than one life. As you progress in the game and encounter challenges of all sorts, you lose a life here and there. But you also earn extra points in a variety of ways, and with enough extra points, you are awarded additional lives. There are also bonus rewards of additional prizes, powers, and abilities that come and go throughout the game.

All of this is very engrossing and motivates the player to continue playing. This intricate system absorbs the player and provides a number of conditions that reward learning: immediate feedback, instant rewards and punishments, hope and desire to see what's around the corner, feelings of accomplishment, and so forth. Finding ways to reward learning in the classroom using similar conditions can really pay off.

Intersperse the Learning with Incentives

Give Previews of Coming Attractions.   Throughout the training, mention interesting and fun activities that are coming up later in the program. Don't overdo this and raise expectations beyond what you can deliver, but occasional simple references to upcoming fun events can be helpful in maintaining interest.

Give Points or Tokens.   Do this throughout the training and at the end of the program have prizes available for a given number of points or tokens.

Toss Treats.   Throw small pieces of candy to people who contribute to discussions, share ideas, solve puzzles first, and so on.

Decorate.   Put ribbons and stickers on participant products. Put ribbons and stickers that say "First Place," "Second Place," and so forth on papers, charts, and wall displays.

Let Participants Judge.   Use participant judges and panels to decide on the "best" projects, ideas, displays, and so forth. They can then make the awards.

Give Audio Rewards and Punishments.   Use gongs or buzzers when participants give wrong answers or fail to meet a deadline. Use positive, "winning" sounds when they give right answers and meet deadlines.

Reward with Time.   Offer rewards of time such as extra lunchtime, longer breaks, or an earlier class ending time for meeting requirements, finishing projects, winning given amounts of points, and so on.

Use Time Punishments.   Have participants lose time (get a shorter lunch or break time) if they miss deadlines, don't finish projects, and so on.

Hand Out Prizes.   Award small prizes for winning games, completing activities, and so on.

the nitty gritty

Creating Sound Effects

Use any of the following items to call class to order, begin and end activities, or administer positive or negative feedback: chimes, gongs, clickers, hand clappers, musical triangle, bells, whistles, tingshas (Tibetan meditation chimes), popping rods (make the sound of a cork coming out of a bottle), battery-operated sound-effects units that make sounds for "right answer," "wrong answer," and "time's up."

USE COMPELLING THEMES AND MOTIFS IN YOUR PROGRAMS

Seminars and training programs often use themes—themes for the entire program or themes for games and activities within the program. A theme well-used can add fun, involvement, and cohesiveness to programs. Themes can be a unifying factor that makes materials more memorable and activities more fun. Let's take a look at some of the favorite themes found in workplace training programs today.

Journey Themes

Journey themes are very common in training and appeal to a wide variety of participants. Within the theme, participants can prepare for their journey, set off on the journey, encounter a variety of obstacles, and, finally, arrive at their destination. Common journey themes include jungle safaris, train trips, cross-country auto trips, sea voyages, flying excursions, and, of course, climbing mountains.

Orientation programs often use journey themes, that is, embarking on a new job/career, but I suggest you consider things like "Climbing to Peak Performance," "Getting Through a Jungle of Customer Complaints," or "Weathering the Rough Seas of Implementing a New System." I'm sure you can think of many others.

Sports Themes

Sports themes are always very popular and are often used for team-building programs and sales training. If particular sports teams are popular with your participants, consider using that team as a theme for a program. Programs with sports themes often have the team working together to overcome adversity and finally winning the big game. The most popular sports theme of the past was football, but with all the national women's teams out there and with so many young women now active in a variety of sports, I suggest you try basketball, baseball and softball, or soccer themes.

Sports themes can be used effectively in other training situations as well. If your program is not team building, consider using more individualistic sports themes such as tennis, golf, swimming, and diving. I can envision "A Day at Wimbleton" for presentation skill building or "Getting into the Swim of Things" for learning a new procedure. I once designed a course on selling your ideas to others called "Hook, Line, and Sinker" that used a fishing theme. What sports themes can you use in your training programs?

Detective, Mystery, and Crime Themes

Detective, mystery, and crime themes are popular for problem-solving programs where participants gather data, discover new information, and solve the problem. The mystery under investigation might be how to increase customer satisfaction or how to lower production costs. The crime could be a dip in quality or any other negative in the workplace that needs to be addressed. Also, consider using a takeoff of a current popular crime or detective TV show like "The Sopranos" or "CSI." Participants can use their own creativity throughout the program.

I have a career development class with a detective theme where I ask participants to think of themselves as detectives investigating themselves. They must gather information, make observations, and assess situations in order to provide themselves with the necessary data to plan their career futures.

Entertainment Themes

Themes taken from television shows, movies, and other types of entertainment can be very effective. Game show themes have long been used in training and development classes, "Jeopardy" and "Who Wants to Be a Millionaire?" being the most popular. But why not try using programs that are popular with the younger generations such as "Survivor," "Joe Millionaire," and other reality shows?

Fantasy Themes

Why not design a game or activity, or perhaps an entire class, that takes a fantasy journey into outer space or through a medieval forest. You can even make use of a "game master." Assign one person per activity group to be the game master. Have all the game masters wear a special hat or a cloak or carry a wand. The game masters can be in charge of maintaining order and enforcing the rules of the activity.

Company-Oriented Themes

Use themes that reflect the nature of the business itself. If the company produces computers, use a computer theme. If the business is a chain of restaurants with a Southwestern theme, use a Southwestern theme for the training.

Combined Themes

Use an outer-space detective theme and have participants gathering information and solving a problem all day in order to save the world. Or how about a survival journey across the desert? Or maybe a soccer team mystery? I'll bet you can come up with a few more.

Other Ways to Use Themes

For group activities, ask each small group to choose a name and a theme for their group and to use that name and theme in their final presentation.

Use themes for board games and card games. Call the game "Sale Soccer," "Merlin's Journey," "Space Evaders," or some such title, and then use appropriate graphics on the game board and/or cards.

Have game boards that are not decorated and ask participants to choose a theme and name for their game board and to decorate it accordingly. You can have stickers, markers, and other materials ready for them.

Put theme graphics on handouts and materials. Nothing too far out or absurd, but an occasional knight in shining armor on a handout about dealing with difficult customers or a slaying-the-dragon icon on a list of ten ways to eliminate defects might work.

the nitty gritty

A Couple of Cool Things to Consider Doing

- Do your own movie trailer, complete with commercials for other courses, and have it playing on the screen before class starts.

- Have an on-screen "quiz" of some type going on before class starts and during breaks. Offer prizes to participants who answer all the questions correctly.

CREATE A RELAXED ENVIRONMENT

One of the surprising things I found in surveying and talking with learners from the younger generation was how often they mentioned a concern for the learning environment. When I asked them to describe the ideal educational class or seminar, sprinkled among a variety of answers were things such as "a comfortable learning environment," "the seminar should not be so serious, but relaxed with drinks and food," "a very relaxed atmosphere," "a laid-back setting," and "in a comfortable room where I could sit on a couch and relax."

Many of their learning experiences in high school and college have been in their rooms at home, in the dorm, or in their shared apartments, where they were very relaxed. Outside of work, these people read and study in bookstores. Many workplaces that employ large numbers of younger workers have fully stocked kitchenettes, lounging areas with sofas and comfortable chairs, and computer games. Why not have learning centers that look like Generation X workplaces? Why not have seminar rooms that mimic popular bookstores with coffee bars and reading corners?

Part of our initial response to ideas like these has to do with cultural differences and perhaps with ownership. Whose seminar is it—the teacher's, the company's, or the students'? Who makes the decisions as to what is learned and how it's learned? Questions like these can lead us into some healthy paradigm shifting, and that's the topic of the next chapter.

● ●

SUMMARY

One of the biggest challenges facing teachers and trainers is to keep learners motivated. Our younger learners have developed habits of studying and learning in relaxed, comfortable environments with learning tools and systems that provide them with immediate feedback and ongoing incentives. We must design and deliver training that engages our learners. We need to infuse our training with learning situations that have high levels of learner involvement, interaction with other learners, and a sense of growing competency. We must design into our training programs plenty of immediate performance feedback and a variety of incentives. We must include games and activities that are challenging, involving, and interactive, and that capture the imagination of our learners. We must incorporate themes and motifs that add fun and enjoyment. And we must make the learning place an enjoyable place to be.

Rattle Your Training Paradigms

Have you ever swapped tales with other trainers comparing your craziest training experiences? You know, like the time the training room you were assigned turned out to be a very large storage closet, but you ended up using it anyway. Or the time during your only experience teaching a third-shift training class that you fell asleep during the break. Or how about the day the training materials didn't make it to the training site and you had to produce training materials on the fly as you went along!

We've all been there and have the tales to prove it. What's intriguing is that these types of experiences are particularly interesting, funny, or appealing because they involve a paradigm shift. We have our preconceived notions of when, where, and how training is done, and when it is otherwise, it makes a good story.

What are your standard paradigms around the design and delivery of training? If they are like mine, your first thoughts turn to time, space, and matter. One-day, two-day, or longer? Six hours or eight? Standard classroom, stand-up delivery, or online e-learning? Technical, soft skills, or industry-specific content? There are variations, of course, but on the whole a very large percentage of the training we do follows "a set of unwritten rules and regulations that define our boundaries and tell us what to do to be successful" (Barker, 1985, p. 32). Sound familiar?

As learning in the workplace becomes more of a constant, ongoing, lifelong phenomenon, diverse approaches will emerge and many of today's paradigms around training and development will expand and transform to meet the needs of the learners of the future. And that future may be just around the corner! Maybe it wouldn't hurt to rattle off few of our favorite training paradigms and see what emerges.

So far, we have looked at numerous adjustments that can be made to make Boomer training more appealing to the emerging generations. We have been addressing the standard way that training is done in today's workplace. We have kept the overall structure, packaging, and macro-designs basically the same while we made simple alterations and revisions in order to pick up the pace, increase interactions, link to the learner, offer options, and make it fun. Let's look at how we might restructure, repackage, and redesign training to better meet the needs of younger learners using different paradigms around time, space, and matter.

● ●

SHIFTING THE TIME, SPACE, AND MATTER OF TRAINING

If you are a fan of Stan Davis, as I have been for many years, you are familiar with his stimulating work *Future Perfect*. Davis writes, "In the industrial economy, managers considered time, space, and matter as constraints, whereas in the new economy they will come to think of them as resources" (Davis, 1987, p. 7). I believe that we trainers of today can facilitate some potentially powerful paradigm shifts in the when, where, and how of training. Certainly, e-learning has done this, but there are other shifts awaiting.

The nine-to-five, one-day or two-day program in the classroom with twenty-four seats in a U-shape, each with a three-ring binder and a name card in place, has already been supplemented with anytime, anyplace online e-learning. However, many of the e-learning programs available are reflections of the normal design and delivery of standard classroom programs. If we apply a variation of the big-three paradigm shifts that Stan Davis presents in *Future Perfect* for the new information economy—anytime, anyplace, no matter—to the field of employee training and development, some interesting ideas arise.

For example, if we change the view of learning time from sometime to anytime to all the time, we can begin to take steps towards "all-the-time" learning. If we change the view of the place and space of learning from some of the space in this place to all the space everyplace, we can begin to take steps to make all of the workplace a learning place. And finally, if we change the concepts of course content and training materials to those of needed knowledge and learning resources, we can take steps to make information, knowledge, and learning resources easily accessible all over the workplace, all of the time. Changes like these could lead to some interesting results. Let's look at a few examples.

● ●

ALL-THE-TIME LEARNING

When we think of "all-the-time learning," it is quite natural to assume that we are discussing e-learning. And electronic learning is a very valid option, but it is not the only all-the-time-learning option. Why not make all types of training available all the time, or at least well beyond the time slots in which most training is presently offered? If you have employees who work at times other than eight to five on weekdays, then learning should be available during all work hours. How many times have you taught a regular nine-to-five training program and noticed a few sleepy second-shift participants? Better yet, how many times have you taught a four-to-midnight second-shift class?

WAYS TO TRAIN WITH A SHIFT OF TIME

- Bring back lunchtime learning and brown-bag lunches.

- Offer training on weeknights and Saturdays with child care included.

- Offer two-hour mini-workshops after work with beer and nachos.

- Offer one-hour mini-workshops before work with coffee, donuts, and fruit.

- Offer in-and-out training. Participants can attend one-hour modules whenever space is available and they are free. For example, I would attend from nine until ten A.M. on Monday, skip Tuesday, sit in on the ten-to-eleven and the eleven-to-twelve sessions on Wednesday, catch the one-to-two session on Friday, and wait until next Tuesday to take the two-to-three and three-to-four segments. When I complete all sessions, I get credit for having taken the course.

- Do away with the concepts of "class" and "time allotments" altogether and offer instant access to a variety of simultaneous learning options—stand-up delivery, e-classes, videos, written materials, and so forth. Learners can pick and choose among these options whenever they like. Learning can employ whatever time it takes.

● ●

ALL THE SPACE EVERYPLACE

Training centers and training rooms are great, but they are not the only place where training can happen. Fill your workplace with learning spaces and learning places. Have "Centers of Learning" or learning locations sprinkled throughout the workplace with
classrooms, study rooms, audiovisual and electronic learning equipment, printed materials, and access to content gurus and expert colleagues. For anyplace learning space, have
rooms in every department and area within the workplace that are designated and dedicated to learning. They can be reserved for individual or group learning events, both for-
mal and informal—just as a room can be reserved for meetings.

Have other employee services available and connected to learning sites so that learners
can learn while chores are done. Put a laundry near the learning center so students can
"wash and learn." Include dinner with evening training programs. And don't forget the
child care facility!

WAYS TO USE ALL OF YOUR LEARNING SPACE

- Include visuals by having charts, graphs, pictures, posters, and cartoons throughout
  the training environment.

- Add sound to your training environment. Play music while people read, surf the
  net, or discuss in small groups.

- Put some movement into the learning space. Hang mobiles from the ceiling. Have
  an aquarium or fishbowl with a few beautiful fish swimming around.

- Put a picture on the ceiling.

● ●

ALL THAT MATTERS

The matter of training has traditionally been printed text with a sprinkling of audiovisual
products such as overhead transparencies and training videos, along with a few games and
activities. The content of these materials is usually agreed on between those doing the design of the materials and those paying for the design of those materials, one hopes with
some input from the eventual receivers of those materials.

Ideas for Design and Delivery of Training Matter

Use Learner Participation in the Design.   Let the learners participate in the design of the learning, not just through a focus group or a series of individual interviews with the target population, but by having members of the target population participate in the design project. Collaboration is the name of the game.

Use Learner-Directed Design.   Have a cadre of "killer designers" and "free-agent facilitators" learners can access for their design and delivery needs. These on-call designers and facilitators would be contracted by the learners to help them design and deliver training that meets the needs and specifications of those learners. The learners would direct how the training would be designed and delivered.

Set Up a Knowledge Distribution System.   Design an on-call knowledge distribution system that uses teachers, trainers, facilitators, mentors, and gurus. Learners would access these learning professionals to gather information and ideas, to facilitate design sessions, to guide learning sessions, and so forth.

Develop a Colleague Expertise Bank.   This would be a listing of employees with their areas of knowledge, experience, and expertise that they have agreed to share in a consulting capacity. Such a list could be accessed when needed.

New Methods to Offer Training Matter

Develop Models.   Use problem-based, engaged learning models that include learning from failure and taking risks.

Offer Collaborative Learning Projects.   Have authentic, real-world, ongoing learning projects that are shared among groups and departments. Have cross-functional learning groups focusing on one particular issue.

Make Learning 24/7.   Offer continuous access to all types of media—printed, electronic, and live.

Have a Learning Games Room.   Make all types of learning games readily available, including a good supply of digital learning games.

Post Information.   Have a learning bulletin board, real or electronic. Employees can post questions, concerns, or even ideas for training programs. When enough people have a need for some type of training, they can form a collaborative learning project, design their own training program, and hire a facilitator.

● ●

FROM TRAINING AS NEEDED TO LIFELONG LEARNING

Another paradigm shift occurring in the world of training and education is the changing role of teacher/trainer to facilitator of learning. The teacher or trainer as the person in charge, the person with the answers, who establishes a procedure or an approach that works and then sticks with it, year after year, is no longer viable. As the learner begins to have more at stake in the learning than the trainer has in the training, the relationship will shift to a more learner-directed event. The trainer will become much more of a facilitator of learning, someone who guides and motivates the learners in their quest for the information and ideas that they need.

In fact, the paradigms of learning and work are also shifting. Learning is moving from being perceived as something you do to prepare for work and then something you do periodically apart from work and come back and perhaps apply to your work. Learning is now becoming a part of the work itself. You don't always know ahead of time what you will need to learn. You find yourself needing to learn as a response to problems and difficult situations. Learning in the workplace is becoming more of a "learn as you go" phenomenon. The attainment of knowledge is constant; thus, the term "lifelong learning."

● ●

SUMMARY

As lifelong learning becomes commonplace and the needs and concerns of workers of all ages change and grow in new directions, fresh approaches to workplace learning will appear. Our paradigms of time, space, and matter in regard to training and development in the workplace will undoubtedly shift and produce more all-the-time, all-the-space-everyplace, and all-that-matters learning.

We can accommodate many of today's learners from the emerging generations by shifting some of those paradigms right now. We can expand learning time by offering learning opportunities in a wider range of time modules and making training available outside the standard eight-to-five workday. We can expand the space of training by setting up learning spaces throughout the workplace and holding training in places that accommodate other trainee needs such as child care.

And finally, the heart of training, the design and delivery systems, can be linked with the learner by adopting learner-directed design and delivery methods. All of these possible changes in the time, space, and matter of training are part of a larger paradigm shift from learning as needed to lifelong learning and from trainers as teachers to trainers as facilitators of learning.

part TWO

Games

This section of the book contains twenty games and activities designed and tested to specifically address the five needs of the emerging generations: pick up the pace, increase interaction, link to the learner, offer options, and make it fun. All can be delivered at a fairly quick pace, and many can be used to start off your program with a bang. They are all interactive—some are highly interactive with participants involved in self-directed discovery. These games are linked to the learners in a variety of ways, including involving them in problem solving, making use of technology, and stimulating their senses. The games have also been designed to offer options and choices, and many can be customized to better fit your learners. Finally, I have built in plenty of fun using everything from bells and whistles to themes and fantasy, prizes and incentives.

● ●

HOW THE GAMES ARE PRESENTED

Each game begins with an icon indicating to what extent each of the five needs of younger learners is met in that particular game. There is also a statement describing the special features of that game, for example, "great way to start a program," "links to learners and gets their input," or "involves learners in solving a problem," and so forth.

The basics of each game are then presented, followed by a step-by-step process for conducting it. I have also included a section called "Prickly Points" after the process, covering issues that I have encountered using the game and suggestions for addressing these issues. For some of the games, I have also included "Variations" that suggest other applications and adaptations of the game.

Finally, let me say that all of these games can be used in a variety of training programs with adult learners of all ages. They are appropriate for use in both the public and private sectors with almost any group of learners. To illustrate the applicability of these games to various training situations, I have used a running example throughout Part Two of how to use each game in a team-building program. This application sample comes at the end of each game.

● ●

HOW THE GAMES ARE ARRANGED

The games are arranged in three categories: those to be used at the beginning of a program, those to be used anywhere within the program, and those to summarize or end the program. Within each of those three categories, the games are listed by the amount of time needed to use them, starting with the shortest and going to the longest.

To help you better find what you need, there is an index on the following pages that lists the games and their various characteristics, such as "good energizer," "uses technology," and "high fun factor." You may also find it helpful to go through the special features section given at the beginning of each game to help you find a game to meet your needs. Of course, the very best way to learn about the games is to go through them one-by-one. So here they are.

Descriptors for the Twenty Games

	Good with Large Groups	Stimulates the Senses	Uses Technology	High Fun Factor	Offers Options, Choices	Good Links to Learners	High Interaction	Picks Up the Pace	Good Energizer	Use as Closing Activity	Use as Opening Activity
Game 1 Sculpt Away		✓	✓	✓	✓	✓	✓	✓	✓	✓	✓
Game 2 Word Search Mania			✓		✓			✓	✓	✓	✓
Game 3 One Hundred Ways		✓	✓	✓		✓	✓	✓		✓	✓
Game 4 A Matter of Definition		✓			✓			✓			✓
Game 5 A Change of View		✓			✓				✓	✓	
Game 6 Royal Flush			✓		✓		✓		✓	✓	
Game 7 Hunt for Examples				✓		✓	✓		✓		

Descriptors for the Twenty Games *(continued)*

	Use as Opening Activity	Use as Closing Activity	Good Energizer	Picks Up the Pace	High Interaction	Good Links to Learners	Offers Options, Choices	High Fun Factor	Uses Technology	Stimulates the Senses	Good with Large Groups
Game 8 Two-Card Audit		✓	✓	✓	✓	✓			✓		
Game 9 Walk the Talk		✓	✓	✓	✓		✓			✓	
Game 10 Find the Top Ten		✓	✓	✓	✓	✓			✓		
Game 11 The Whole Is Greater		✓	✓	✓	✓	✓	✓	✓	✓		
Game 12 A Stick by Any Other Name		✓	✓	✓	✓		✓		✓		
Game 13 Online Treasure Hunt		✓	✓	✓	✓	✓		✓			
Game 14 Generational Bingo		✓	✓	✓	✓		✓		✓		

	Use as Opening Activity	Use as Closing Activity	Good Energizer	Picks Up the Pace	High Interaction	Good Links to Learners	Offers Options, Choices	High Fun Factor	Uses Technology	Stimulates the Senses	Good with Large Groups
Game 15 Q&A Black Jack		✓	✓	✓			✓		✓		
Game 16 Approach and Coach			✓	✓	✓			✓			
Game 17 Ready, Set, Goal		✓	✓	✓	✓	✓					
Game 18 Involve to Solve				✓	✓	✓		✓			
Game 19 Across the Board	✓	✓		✓	✓	✓	✓		✓		
Game 20 Jelly Bean Art	✓	✓	✓			✓	✓		✓		

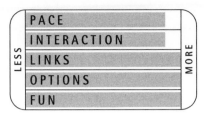

PACE		
INTERACTION		
LINKS		
OPTIONS		
FUN		

LESS   MORE

game **1**

Sculpt Away

Group Size: 6 to 20

Time Required: 45 to 60 minutes with discussions

Special Features: It is surprising how much people enjoy this involving, hands-on, fun activity. It's a great way to start off a program and start people talking about the subject matter.

Summary: Participants are given sculpting dough as they arrive in class and compete to produce the prettiest, funniest, and ugliest sculptures; then, in small groups, they produce sculptures that represent some aspect or characteristic of an effective leader. Finally, they all work together to produce a sculpture that represents effective leadership.

Goals: To begin discussions of effective leadership and to provide an opportunity for leadership to arise

Materials

● One small can of modeling dough for each participant

● One large can of modeling dough for each small group

● A large amount of modeling dough (at least six cans) for the final whole-group activity

● Many cardboard squares of various sizes on which to set the sculptures

● Six small prizes and one large prize that can be shared

● A large, loud timer

● Digital camera (optional)

Physical Setting: Any classroom or meeting-room setting

● ●

PROCESS

1. Give each participant a small can of modeling dough and a small cardboard square as they arrive for the class. Tell them to start sculpting anything they like and that there will be prizes later for the prettiest, the funniest, and the ugliest sculptures.

2. When it's time for class to begin, let people who have a finished product hold up their sculptures. Let the class vote on the three categories, then hand out prizes.

3. Next, divide the participants into groups of four and give each group a large can of modeling dough. Tell them they have ten minutes to sculpt something that portrays an attribute of an effective leader. Say that prizes will be given for the most creative, the most accurate, and the most unusual sculptures.

4. Show the class the timer you are going to use and put it where they can see it and hear it, then let them begin creating their sculptures.

5. When the timer goes off, have all groups put their artwork on display on a table at the front of the room. Ask representatives from each small group to step forward and explain their sculpture to the whole group, including the concept or characteristic of leadership that they chose and why they chose it.

6. As groups explain their sculptures, make a list of their chosen characteristics on a flip chart. After the last presentation, have the group discuss the list and what other characteristics they think should be added. Let them vote on the three most important characteristics of a good leader.

7. Next, have the group look at the sculptures again and decide which groups should receive which prizes. Distribute the prizes.

8. Finally, have all of the groups combine into one large group and give them a large amount of sculpting dough. Tell them they have ten minutes to create a final sculpture that represents what they think is the most important aspect of an effective leader. Set the timer and put it where they can see it and hear it.

9. As the members of the group work together to create their sculpture, observe their interactions and take notes that you can use during the debriefing of this activity. Pay particular attention to their own use of the attributes or characteristics of effective leaders that they have just voted on as being the most important.

10. When the timer goes off, have everybody stop, stand back, and look at their creation. Lots of good debriefing and discussion can follow this. Some debriefing questions might be

   • What happened? How did you decide what to make?

   • How did you accomplish this task?

   • What roles did people take? How were roles decided?

   • Were there leaders who emerged?

   • Which effective characteristics were missing?

   • What did you learn?

   • How can you use what you learned back at work?

11. Put their final sculpture somewhere prominent in the room and display all of their other sculptures around the room.

12. Take digital pictures of their artwork and post the pictures on your website.

PRICKLY POINTS

- Have plenty of extra modeling dough available. Sometimes a small group or the entire group have a fantastic idea they want to implement, but they need more dough.

- The cardboard squares are important. Some modeling dough leaves greasy stains; plus, the cardboard makes it easier to move the sculptures.

- Sometimes people have difficulty coming up with ideas of what to sculpt for something that portrays an attribute of an effective leader and you may have to make suggestions or generate a list of possibilities with them. Some ideas include a person with his right hand on his heart and his left hand raised to indicate honesty or truthfulness; a heart to indicate caring; a brain to indicate intelligence; a person being followed by other people to illustrate that a leader must have followers; and so forth.

VARIATIONS

- Just the opening part of this activity can be an effective warm-up activity. When participants arrive, they can receive some modeling dough and begin to work on a sculpture representing a characteristic of effective leadership. Once class begins, there can be a quick review of the sculptures and an awarding of prizes.

- The opening activity can be deleted, and this can just be used as a regular activity at any point in a training program. Divide the participants into small groups, give them the modeling dough, and ask them to sculpt representations of characteristics of effective leadership.

- This activity can be used for other topics, not only for leadership. Try it for effective teams, ways to raise employee morale, qualities of good customer service, designs for new products or product enhancements, and so forth.

TEAM-BUILDING EXAMPLE

This activity works very well with team-building classes. Assign participants to sculpt something that portrays a characteristic of an effective team. During the activity, look for effective team characteristics being displayed (or not being displayed) by participants and use that for discussion. If the class is made up entirely of one work group or work team, the final activity can be used to analyze how the team works together.

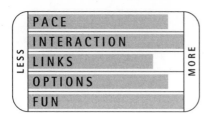

	PACE		
LESS	INTERACTION		MORE
	LINKS		
	OPTIONS		
	FUN		

Word Search Mania

Group Size: 6 to 60

Time Required: 30 minutes

Special Features: Encountering a wall filled with word search puzzles and being able to work on them immediately gets things off to a fun start and has participants interacting and thinking about the subject matter right away.

Summary: In this wall-poster word-search game, participants quickly search for words that relate to the qualities of a good leader, list those words, and write down how and why they relate to a good leader.

Goal: To discuss the qualities of a good leader

Materials

- Four to six large wall posters of the leadership word search puzzle

- Masking tape

- Large sheets of paper posted next to the wall posters

- Highlighting markers in different colors

- Pens and pencils

- A large, loud timer

- Word search answers handout

- Three large prizes that can be shared among group members

- Four to six small prizes

Physical Setting: Enough wall space to hang the word search posters and be able to have a few blank papers hanging to the side of them

● ●

PROCESS

Before the Program

1. Make copies of the leadership word search puzzle on large, colorful wall posters. You will want to assign three or four people to each poster, so four posters will do for classes of around sixteen people, but you will need five or six posters for larger groups. Use masking tape to hang the posters around the room and place a large, blank sheet of white paper next to each.

2. Make copies of the word search answers handout and have them ready to use at the end of this activity.

During the Program

1. As participants arrive, give them highlighting markers and pens or pencils and assign them to one of the large word search posters. Divide the group into small

groups by assigning the first person to arrive to poster number one, the next to poster number two, and so forth, thus eventually forming groups at each poster. Tell them to find words that describe the qualities of a good leader and draw lines through those words.

2. Explain that the large sheets of paper hanging on each side of the posters are for recording the words that they mark on the word search poster. They must list each word they have marked, along with an explanation of how that word relates to good leadership.

3. Tell participants that each group will receive one point for each word and explanation. The more words, the more points; the group with the most points will win a prize.

4. When everyone has arrived, tell the participants that they have five minutes more to find as many words as possible. Set a timer and put it where they can see it. If groups start to slow down, encourage them to keep looking for words. Soon it should become obvious that all sorts of words can somehow be related to leadership.

5. When the timer goes off, have the participants find seats. Distribute the answers handout and go over it.

6. Then have participants share and defend the additional words they have generated. Award the large prizes to the group that found the most words and the smaller prizes to groups with words and definitions that were the biggest stretch, the most poignant, and so forth.

7. End the activity by having participants choose what they consider to be the five most important characteristics of a good leader.

8. Debrief with questions like:

   • What happened?

   • Did you have trouble finding words?

   • How did you respond to the time pressure?

   • What important words were not in the puzzle?

   • What did you learn?

   • How can you use what you learned?

PRICKLY POINTS

- Try not to hang the wall charts too close together. It is better to put them in different places around the room. This makes it more difficult to see what other groups are finding.

- If you construct your own word searches, include as many descriptors as possible, but also be sure to include some neutral or funny words that can stimulate some unusual descriptors. I have seen some excellent generational differences given to words like neat, cool, and hot.

VARIATIONS

- This activity can work with a variety of topics, such as characteristics of effective teams, descriptors of effective feedback, qualities of an effective presentation, and so on. Just choose your topic and generate a word search puzzle. For a website that helps you generate word searches, see The Puzzle Maker section on Discoveryschool.com.

TEAM-BUILDING EXAMPLES

This activity works well with team-building classes. Construct a word search using characteristics of effective teams that reflects the content of your program. During the activity, look for effective team characteristics being displayed, or not being displayed, by participants and use that for discussion.

Leadership Characteristics Word Search

A	X	Y	E	S	T	R	O	N	G	D	C	A	R	I	N	G	P
P	L	H	N	C	A	E	B	N	I	E	U	C	C	O	O	L	R
P	C	T	E	I	L	M	E	R	B	N	T	O	D	O	E	A	O
R	I	R	R	T	L	P	I	E	L	I	E	U	D	A	R	N	U
O	T	O	G	S	O	A	F	U	N	M	O	R	S	M	E	O	D
A	A	W	E	A	F	T	F	O	J	R	A	A	Y	R	C	I	T
C	M	T	T	I	E	H	E	U	P	E	N	G	L	I	N	T	N
H	S	S	I	S	T	G	S	A	T	T	E	E	E	F	I	A	A
A	I	U	C	U	U	T	T	D	S	E	R	O	V	T	S	R	G
B	R	R	R	H	C	I	R	O	E	D	T	U	I	I	X	N	O
L	A	T	W	T	E	M	A	O	N	A	S	S	L	D	T	I	R
E	H	K	I	N	D	I	M	G	O	E	C	I	N	Y	O	C	R
A	C	E	T	E	V	D	S	I	H	T	O	U	G	H	H	E	A

See if you can find these words (and perhaps a few others):

APPROACHABLE	GOOD	PATIENT
CARING	HONEST	PLEASANT
CHARISMATIC	JUST	SMART
ENERGETIC	KIND	STRONG
ENTHUSIASTIC	NICE	TRUSTWORTHY
FAIR	OPEN	TRUTHFUL

	LESS		MORE
PACE			
INTERACTION			
LINKS			
OPTIONS			
FUN			

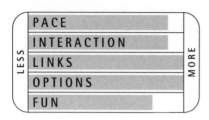

game 3

One Hundred Ways

Group Size: 6 to 30

Time Required: 40 minutes

Special Features: Link to your learners, stimulate their senses, and give them lots of choices by involving them in this creative group project.

Summary: Participants create a huge wall mural illustrating one hundred ways to address a problem.

Goal: To generate ideas

Materials

- Large sheets of white paper, enough to cover a surface at least three or four feet by five or six feet

- Masking tape

- Old magazines, scissors, paste, colored markers, paper

- Computers with access to the Internet and connected to a printer

- A tape player and music

- A prize for each participant when the one hundred ideas are reached

- A flip chart and markers

- A large, loud timer

Physical Setting: Enough wall space to put up paper for a mural

● ●

PROCESS

Before the Program

1. Use masking tape to cover a large section of the classroom wall with thick white paper. Cover a surface at least three or four feet high by five or six feet wide. At the top center of the paper, write, "One Hundred Ways to . . ." and fill in the topic you are using. For example, use phrases like "one hundred ways to raise employee morale," "one hundred ways to improve customer service," or "one hundred ways to market our new fruit drinks."

2. On a small table near the mural lay out a number of old magazines, scissors, paste, markers, construction paper, and similar items. On another table near the mural have a few computers with Internet access that are connected to a printer.

During the Program

1. As people arrive for class, give them colored markers and ask them to begin working on the mural. Say that they can draw pictures, write words, use quotations, cut out pictures from magazines and paste them on the mural, access information and pictures from the Internet and print them out—whatever works for them. Have music playing.

2. When all participants have arrived and it is time to start, announce that they can take another ten minutes to work on the mural and then they will have to take their seats. Say that if they succeed in putting one hundred ideas on the mural, they will all receive a prize.

3. Set a timer and place it where they can see it and hear it. As the time goes by, encourage someone to count the ideas and let the other participants know how close they are.

4. When the timer goes off, ask everyone to stop and help you count the number of ideas on the mural. If they have reached one hundred ideas or more, give them prizes.

5. Ask the participants to form small groups and give them five minutes to choose what they think are the three best ideas on the mural.

6. When five minutes are up, have the groups report out as you list their ideas on a flip chart. Go through the list and pick out the three to five ideas that appear most often. Mark these ideas and explain that they will be using these ideas during the day as you all work on addressing the problem situation.

7. Explain that, throughout the day, people should add further ideas and illustrations to the mural. If they haven't already reached one hundred ideas, say that when they do reach that number, everyone will receive a prize.

8. Debrief by asking questions such as:

   • Why do you think I had you draw the mural?

   • Which items on our list do you think are most important?

   • How can we use this information in our class today?

● ●

PRICKLY POINTS

● It helps if the prizes are attractive and are out in sight.

● If you use this as an opening activity in the morning, make the prizes some type of breakfast snack. (See the Nitty Gritty box on Early Morning Prizes under Game 4, A Matter of Definition.)

Variations

- You may have to give smaller groups more time to reach one hundred ideas.

- Although it makes a good opening exercise, this activity can work well at any time. It also makes a good afternoon energizing activity.

TEAM-BUILDING EXAMPLE

Use this activity to help team members generate ideas to address problems facing the team.

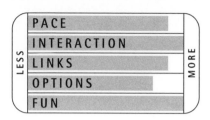

	PACE	
LESS	INTERACTION	MORE
	LINKS	
	OPTIONS	
	FUN	

game 4

A Matter of Definition

Group Size: 4 to 100 or more

Time Required: 15 to 20 minutes

Special Features: This activity can be used for almost any type of class. It gets participants up, moving around the room, and immediately interacting with course material.

Summary: When participants arrive, they are given copies of a quiz to work on and asked to walk around the room reading definition posters on the wall and looking at cartoons and pictures that illustrate the subject matter in order to determine the right answers to the quiz and win a prize.

Goal: To review definitions relevant to course content

Materials

- Copies of a twenty-item quiz pertinent to the program

- Posters with relevant definitions and examples

- Posters with relevant cartoons, illustrations, and quotations

- Masking tape

- Tape/CD player with lively music

- Enough small prizes for every participant

- A large, loud timer

- A flip chart and markers

Physical Setting: Typical classroom with wall space for hanging plenty of posters

PROCESS

Before the Program

1. Construct a twenty-item quiz based on definitions and examples of key concepts relevant to your program. Make it long enough to take at least ten minutes to answer and difficult enough that participants will need to spend time thinking about some of the items and perhaps discussing them with other participants. You may want to include one or two items that have no specific right answer, but will lead to good discussion. For these types of items, any answer would be considered a "right" answer. You may also want to include a few funny or unusual items as well.

2. Construct posters with definitions of key concepts from the program and other posters with cartoons and illustrations of key concepts, and use masking tape to hang them on the walls around the room. See if you can find quotes from famous people about the subject matter and have these displayed as well.

During the Program

1. As participants arrive, give them copies of the quiz to take. Tell them to walk around the room, read the posters, and look at the cartoons and illustrations to obtain information that will help them with the quiz. Tell them to introduce themselves to each other and discuss the quiz. They can work with other participants in groups if they like. Have music playing.

2. When all participants have arrived and/or it is time to start the class, announce that people can take five more minutes to answer their quizzes. Encourage them to share answers and work together. Tell them there will be prizes for anyone who has all the right answers! Set a timer and put it where they can see it and hear it.

3. When the timer goes off, turn off the music and ask participants to return to their seats. Go over the questions and answers. Let participants share their answers and their reasoning.

4. Record key comments on a flip chart as they are made and note areas of concern. These will be useful to you throughout the rest of your training.

5. When all questions and answers have been thoroughly discussed, award prizes to all the participants who had "perfect" papers.

6. Debrief with these questions:

   • Which questions were easy?

   • Which questions were difficult?

   • Why did we do this activity?

7. Introduce the class objectives and show how the quiz and the posters around the room tie into the class content.

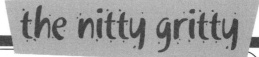

Early Morning Prizes

- Small boxes of raisins, cereal bars, granola bars, apples, bananas, pears, cold cans or boxes of juice

PRICKLY POINTS

- Much of the success of this activity depends on the effort you put into the quiz and the wall posters. Make the quiz cover important definitions and concepts. Also make sure that it touches on key issues and problems within the subject matter.

- Use commercially available posters that illustrate key concepts, but also construct your own posters using pictures and interesting quotations. If this is a class you teach often, you can build and develop your poster collection over time.

- As an example, for a class on selling your ideas to others, I collected a number of pictures used in popular advertising that illustrated key concepts covered in the class. It was a two-day class and on the second day half a dozen participants brought in pictures they had found that illustrated concepts.

- The material that you have hanging on the walls can also be used throughout the training program and is thus a nice unifying factor. It is good to use as part of the summarizing at the end of the program.

TEAM-BUILDING EXAMPLE

To use this game in a team-building course, gather lots of pictures and posters illustrating the characteristics of effective teams. You can also put up posters of local men's and women's sports teams. Have other charts and posters that give information on how effective teams help the organization. If the group is all from the same team, let them spend the last five minutes of this activity working together. You can take notes on how they work together and use the information in the debriefing and later on in the class.

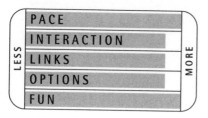

	PACE	
	INTERACTION	
LESS	LINKS	MORE
	OPTIONS	
	FUN	

game 5

A Change of View

Group Size: 10 to 100 or more

Time Required: 5 minutes

Special Features: This quick, easy energizer can really pick up the pace. It's perfect for when the mid-afternoon lull begins. It's also nice to use when you have participants you want to move elsewhere.

Summary: Participants are asked to pick up all of their belongings and move to a new seat. They have only 30 seconds to do so, but receive a small prize if they accomplish it.

Goals: To get everyone up and moving, to meet different people, and to gain new perspectives

Materials

- A basket or bowl filled with small, edible prizes for everyone

- A loud, ticking timer

Physical Setting: Typical classroom or seminar set-up

● ●

PROCESS

1. Stop what you are doing, pause, and look around. Tell the group that you feel the need for a change. Ask participants to pick up all of their belongings and prepare to move to a new seat. Take out a bowl or basket of small, edible prizes, and let them see it.

2. Inform them that when you say so, they should stand and move to a new seat. The new seat cannot be a seat that is next to the seat they are now in.

3. Tell them they have thirty seconds to move to their new seats and that you will throw a prize to anyone in a new seat before the time is up. Anyone not in a new seat by the end of the thirty seconds won't receive a prize!

4. Show them the timer, set it, and say, "Go." As people take new seats, throw out prizes.

5. Let participants know when there are only ten seconds to go. In fact, count out the last ten seconds as you walk around throwing prizes at the last few seat-taking participants.

6. When all participants are seated, tell them to turn and introduce themselves to any new neighbors that they haven't met yet today.

7. Do a very short debriefing, asking questions such as:

   - Why did I do this activity?

   - How do things look from your new seats?

   - Do you see anything differently?

   - What are the advantages of changing your literal point of view?

PRICKLY POINTS

- It's best to approach this activity in an upbeat manner and do it quickly and matter-of-factly. Don't give people a chance to moan and groan or bargain.

- If you use this activity to break up pairs or small groups, you can add a rule about not sitting next to anyone they are sitting next to now. Put a "meet new people" twist on it.

TEAM-BUILDING EXAMPLE

This is a good activity to use with very large teams where small cliques have begun to form and you want to break them up. It also works nicely in programs with a number of teams included where you want the various teams to mix more.

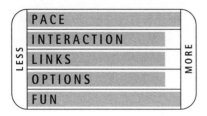

PACE
INTERACTION
LINKS
OPTIONS
FUN

LESS | MORE

game 6

Royal Flush

Group Size: 10 to 30

Time Required: 15 minutes

Special Features: This energizing activity picks up the pace and is a lively, fun way to form groups. It can also be used to illustrate the effects of wanting to win on individual and group behavior.

Summary: Each participant receives a playing card and the class is given five minutes to form groups of five to seven people. When the groups are formed, the group with the highest-scoring poker hand wins a prize.

Goals: To form small groups and to observe the effects of "wanting to win" on individual and group behavior

Materials

- A deck of playing cards
- A poster of winning poker hands
- A nice, big prize that can be easily shared
- A large, loud timer

Physical Setting: Regular training room

● ●

PROCESS

Before the Program

1. Construct a stack of playing cards that contains only one Ace of Hearts, one King of Hearts, one Queen of Hearts, one Jack of Hearts, one Ten of Hearts, one Nine of Hearts, one King of Diamonds, one King of Spades, one King of Clubs, one Ten of Clubs, and as many other cards of lower denominations (nine and under) as needed to equal the number of participants in the activity. Shuffle the stack.

2. Construct and post at the front of the classroom a large chart that gives the different winning hands in poker, as listed at the end of this game.

During the Program

1. Tell the participants that you want them to form small groups. Ideally, you would like them to form groups of five, but if necessary, they can have six or seven people in a group. *No group should be larger than seven people and every participant must be in a group.*

2. Explain that you will soon give every participant a playing card and that if they can form a group that has cards equal to a Royal Flush, they will win a prize. Set the prize out for all to see. Explain further that if no group has cards equal to a Royal Flush, then the prize will go to the group with the next-highest-scoring poker hand.

3. Point out the chart on the wall that gives the different winning hands in poker and ask if there are any questions.

4. Give the participants a moment to look over the chart and then start distributing cards, one per participant. Tell people they have five minutes to stand up, move around, and begin forming teams. Set the timer and put it where all can see and hear.

5. When the timer goes off, call out for them to stop, then check to see which group has the highest poker hand and award them the prize.

6. Debrief by asking the following questions:

   • What happened?

   • How did the card you have affect your actions?

   • Were you able to meet the goal?

   • What did you learn by doing this activity?

   • How can you use this information in the workplace in the future?

PRICKLY POINTS

• Conduct this activity at a fairly quick pace. Don't give people too much time to plan and plot. Pass out the cards, set the timer, and let them go.

• In general, this activity is a nice, quick, unusual way to divide the class into groups, but it can present other dynamics.

• There will sometimes be one or two poker enthusiasts in the group who will really want to win. Depending on group dynamics and your goals for the program, you may want to either play up or play down their actions. I have seen groups struggle to win by finding the exact cards they needed, only to run out of time and lose because they were so focused on bringing people with very specific cards into their group.

TEAM-BUILDING EXAMPLE

In a team-building program, this activity can illustrate working for your individual team to win versus working for all of the teams to win. It can elicit discussions around questions like: If there's not much time, is it better for your team to win and other company teams to lose? Or is it better to work together and risk the chance of all teams losing? Or are there other options to work toward?

Poker Hands: Arranged Highest to Lowest

Royal Flush: A, K, Q, J, 10 all of the same suit

Straight Flush: Any five-card sequence in the same suit (Example: 8, 9, 10, J, Q or A, 2, 3, 4, 5 of same suit)

Four of a Kind: All four cards of same index (Example: K, K, K, K)

Full House: Three of a kind combined with a pair (Example: A, A, A, 5, 5)

Flush: Any five cards of the same suit, but not in sequence

Straight: Five cards in sequence, but not in the same suit

Three of a Kind: Three cards of the same index

Two Pair: Two separate pairs (Example 4, 4, Q, Q)

Pair: Two cards of the same index

PACE		MORE
INTERACTION		
LINKS		
OPTIONS		
FUN		

LESS

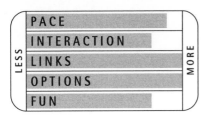

A Hunt for Examples

Group Size: 5 to 100

Time Required: 30 minutes

Special Features: Link to your learners, offer them options, and test their understanding in this simple online activity that has them hunting for examples.

Summary: Participants have fifteen minutes to search for examples that illustrate a key course concept by going online or using other resources.

Goal: To have participants demonstrate understanding of a key concept

Materials

- Eight or more copies of current magazines
- Computers with online access and printers

- Many small prizes

- A large, loud timer

- One "grand prize"

Physical Setting: A room with computers that have online access

• •

PROCESS

Before the Program

1. Select a particular concept from the course that you want to reinforce. Gather a number of magazines and printed resources that are likely to have articles or pictures that illustrate the concept and place them on a table in the classroom.

2. Have computers with Internet access available for use and connected to a printer so that participants can print copies of examples they find.

During the Program

1. After the chosen concept has been covered in the program, tell the participants that you would like them to quickly find good examples of that concept.

2. Show them the magazines that are arranged on the table and point out the computers that are available. Tell them that each of them must find an example that illustrates the concept. They may go online and print out examples or go through the magazines and find examples.

3. Tell them they have fifteen minutes to accomplish this and that anyone who finds an example within the fifteen-minute period will win a prize.

4. Set the timer and place it in area where the participants can see and hear it.

5. When the timer goes off, reconvene the group and let people share their examples. After each example is given, ask the group if they agree that it is a valid example of the concept. If they agree that it is, give that person a prize and have the next person with an example come forward.

6. After all examples have been given, let the group determine which was the best example and award that person the "grand prize."

7. Debrief the activity with questions such as:

- What happened? How did you prefer to find examples?

- What examples do you particularly like and why?

PRICKLY POINTS

- As participants actively seek out examples, walk around and encourage their efforts. When someone shows you an example, give him or her positive reinforcement for the effort. If a particular example is not too good, explain why and encourage the person to keep on looking.

- If you have a large group and not enough computers, you could give them another five or ten minutes to do the activity or let them work in groups.

VARIATIONS

- Instead of examples, have participants look for interesting quotes, good definitions, or ways to do something.

TEAM-BUILDING EXAMPLE

Let teams work together to find ten examples of a concept. You can monitor how the teams work together and give them feedback on that as well as on the actual examples they come up with.

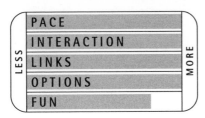

Two-Card Audit

Group Size: 6 to 30

Time Required: 30 to 40 minutes

Special Features: Use this energizing activity to link to your learners and obtain their input about how the course is going by asking them to share information on what is going well with the program and what they still hope to learn.

Summary: Participants write something useful they have learned in the program on a card and something they still want to know on a different card and then mix and mingle, sharing and analyzing the information on the cards. They then determine the top three things that people have learned and the top three things that people still want to learn.

Goal: To have participants audit how the learning is going

Materials

- Two sets of index cards in different colors

- Pens and pencils

- A whistle

- A flip chart or white board and the appropriate markers

Physical Setting: An open space where participants can mix and mingle

● ●

PROCESS

1. Loudly flip through a stack of blank file cards to get the attention of the participants. Tell them it is time for a short class audit.

2. Quickly distribute blank file cards of one color and pens or pencils to participants and ask them to write down one thing that they have learned thus far in the program that will be useful to them.

3. Next, flip through another stack of blank cards, these of a different color, and distribute them to participants. Ask them to write down something they still want to learn about or discuss during the remainder of the program.

4. Now have the participants stand, take their two cards, and go to an open area. Explain that they will have ten minutes to mix and mingle and discuss with one another what they have written on their two cards.

5. Tell them that there's not much time and you want them to speak with as many people as possible, so you are going to use a whistle to keep things moving.

6. Say that when you blow the whistle, they should form small groups of two or three people and discuss their cards. When you blow the whistle again, they should move on and form new groups and discuss their cards. This will continue until the ten minutes are up.

7. Blow the whistle and let them form groups. Let them talk for a minute or two and then blow the whistle. Continue to do this until the ten minutes are up, at which point you can blow the whistle two or three times and ask everyone to stop talking and return to their seats.

8. Have two volunteer participants gather up the cards, one color at a time. Then divide the participants into two groups and give one deck of cards to each group.

9. Tell them they have ten minutes to sort their cards and choose, according to which deck they have, either the top three things that people have learned or the top three things that people still want to learn about or discuss.

10. As they determine their top three, have the groups list their three items on a flip chart or on a white board.

11. When time is up, blow the whistle and ask for a spokesperson from each group to share their top items.

12. Debrief the entire activity with questions such as:

   • What happened?

   • How easy or difficult was it to find cards that were similar?

   • Do you all pretty much agree on the items posted?

   • How can we use what was learned from this activity?

• •

PRICKLY POINTS

   ● This is meant to be a quick audit and needs to be done quickly. Too much thinking, writing, and discussing leads to over-analysis and a focus on course design rather than a focus on what they've learned and still want to learn.

   ● When I've used this activity, I've noticed that there are always a few people who are overly eager to critique the entire course or they like to write cute answers such as, "I've learned to get to the refreshments early before the best donuts are gone." It helps to mention such tendencies before they begin and emphasize that this is just a quick checking-in activity regarding the learning that has occurred.

   ● Collect the cards at the end of this activity. They are a very valuable source of information for you.

VARIATIONS

● Use this game to audit other aspects of the program. To obtain feedback on a particular game or activity, you could ask what they liked and did not like or what the game needs more of or less of.

TEAM-BUILDING EXAMPLE

Use this activity to audit how a team meeting is going, how a project is coming along, or how team members feel about a training program they are attending.

	LESS		MORE
PACE			
INTERACTION			
LINKS			
OPTIONS			
FUN			

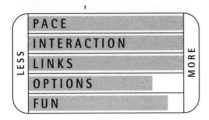

game 9

Walk the Talk

Group Size: Any group of 24 or more

Time Required: 20 to 30 minutes

Special Features: Pick up the pace and involve learners with this novel large-group activity.

Summary: Participants in a large lecture hall form pairs to discuss questions that have been projected and then form small groups of four to discuss the questions further while the instructor walks around listening in on the discussions and giving away candy.

Goal: To give an opportunity for discussion in a large group

Materials

- A large screen and a projector for presenting discussion questions to the group

- A loud whistle or gong

- A large bag of individually wrapped candies

Physical Setting: Any large-group setting

• •

PROCESS

1. During a lecture to a large group, stop at some point and ask a rhetorical question. Then say, "That really is a pretty good question. I'd like for you to discuss that question!"

2. Ask everyone in the audience to find a partner. Tell them to turn and talk to someone beside them or perhaps in front of them or behind them.

3. Project the question on the screen and say that they have five minutes to discuss the question. If they can't find a partner, they should join two other people and form a group of three. The main point is to talk to someone about the question.

4. When five minutes are over, blow a whistle or sound a gong to reconvene the group.

5. Ask the audience to now form small groups of four people. Say that they will have ten minutes to continue discussing the next question that you are projecting on the screen. Project the next question while they are forming groups of four.

6. As the small groups discuss the next question, you can walk among the participants. Carry a large bag of candy with you. As you go from group to group, listen to their discussions and reward good comments and good discussions with candy.

7. Don't stay with any group too long; keep walking about. When you hear individuals make good comments as you are walking about, throw them pieces of candy.

8. Work your way around the room and then back up to the front.

9. When the ten minutes are over, blow a whistle or sound a gong to reconvene the group. Before you begin your lecture again, thank them for their discussions and contributions and throw the remaining candy out into the audience.

● ●

PRICKLY POINTS

● Keep it snappy. Walk around at a good pace and cover most of the room if possible.

● Depending on the design of the room and how much space there is, you may not be able to listen to very many discussions, but you can still reward good participation when you see it.

TEAM–BUILDING EXAMPLE

If you have a large number of teams meeting together for some type of presentation or event, this can be used as a way of encouraging them to talk and discuss issues with people from different teams.

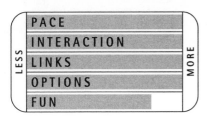

PACE
INTERACTION
LINKS
OPTIONS
FUN

LESS   MORE

game 10

Find the Top Ten

Group Size: 6 to 24

Time Required: 30 to 40 minutes

Special Features: Pick up the pace and raise energy levels with this quick consensus-reaching activity.

Summary: Participants use a card-sorting activity to generate what they feel are the top ten problems, reasons for a problem, or ways to improve a situation posed by the instructor.

Goal: To reach a quick consensus

Materials

● Three blank three-by-five index cards for each participant

- Pens or pencils
- A loud timer
- A large table that participants can stand around
- Flip chart and markers
- Prizes

Physical Setting: A large open space for all participants to mix and mingle

PROCESS

1. Distribute three blank index cards and a pen or pencil to each participant and instruct them to write what they believe to be three reasons or causes for the problem being discussed. They should put each reason on a separate card.

2. Ask participants to bring their cards with them and come over to an open area.

3. Now ask participants to mix and mingle and share and discuss their cards with one another. Explain that they only have ten minutes to do this and so they should try to talk to as many people as possible.

4. Set the timer and place it where they can see it and hear it.

5. When the timer goes off, have participants bring their cards to the large table and spread them out on the table, written side up.

6. Tell the participants that they will have fifteen minutes to sort through the cards, arrange them into categories, and determine which causes or reasons have been selected the most. Then they should decide on the top ten causes or reasons for the problem and write them on a flip chart.

7. Say that if they can accomplish all of that in the fifteen minutes, they will all receive a prize. Explain that you will set the timer for fifteen minutes, and when it goes off they must stop.

8. Set the timer and place it where they can see it and hear it. When the timer goes off, call a halt to their activity. If they have accomplished the task, award them the prizes.

9. Discuss their results and debrief the activity using the following questions:

- How easy was it to find cards that listed the same reasons?

- What do you think of your final top ten reasons?

- What can you do to improve things now that you know about the reasons?

PRICKLY POINTS

- This activity works well in situations where there is a fair amount of common knowledge about the situation or problem, but you do not want to spend large amounts of time going over all of that. It allows the group to zero in on key issues quickly.

- If you have some very dominant participants, you can divide the whole group into two groups for the second part of the activity. Use your best judgment to either split up the dominant people or put the very dominant participants together in one group. Either way, there will be more opportunity for everyone to participate and have their ideas included. You can then combine the final lists in some way.

VARIATIONS

- If you want to narrow the results down further, go for the top five or the big seven.

- This activity can take place online before a class or a meeting. Have participants send you their three reasons or causes by e-mail. You can then construct a list of all the reasons and causes. Send these to all the participants and have them choose their top ten and send them back to you. You can bring the results to the class or meeting and use them for problem-solving or brainstorming activities.

TEAM-BUILDING EXAMPLE

This activity is especially effective with teams. It can be used in a variety of team situations where quick consensus-building is needed. It also provides a way to tap into the ideas and opinions of quieter team members. It can also be very energizing.

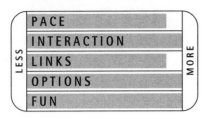

	PACE	
	INTERACTION	
LESS	LINKS	MORE
	OPTIONS	
	FUN	

game 11

The Whole Is Greater

Group Size: 12 to 24

Time Required: 45 minutes

Special Features: If you need a simple, enjoyable activity that involves learners in solving a problem, this is it.

Summary: In this hands-on activity, small groups first use tangram* puzzles to create rectangles, then pictures, and finally the groups combine and work together using all of their puzzles to create one large picture.

Goal: To experience the difficulties of working on a large-group project

*A tangram is a puzzle of Chinese origin that involves putting together seven pieces, usually a square, a parallelogram, and five triangles, to form different shapes.

Materials

- One tangram puzzle for each small group, in separate bags

- A digital camera, a computer, and a printer (optional)

- A large, loud timer

- Three small prizes that can be shared by small groups

- One large prize that can be shared by the whole class

Physical Setting: Enough table space for small groups to work with the puzzles and a large table or tables that can be pushed together for the entire group to stand around

the nitty gritty

Websites for Tangrams

- www.tangram.i-p.com—This website lets you do an interactive tangram puzzle. It also has a master stencil that you can print out and use, as well as samples of pictures you can make with the puzzle.

- www.areyougame.com—There are lots of puzzles that you can buy on this website, including tangrams.

- www.enchantdmind.com/puzzles/tangram—This puzzle and creativity site has an interactive tangram puzzle.

- www.terragame.com—This site sells a 3-D tangram game for Windows.

- www.strongmuseum.org/kids/tangram.html—This site of the Strong Museum in Rochester, New York, has a good model of the tangram puzzle that you can print out and use to make your own puzzles. It also has a nice selection of pictures for children to make.

• •

PROCESS

1. Divide the participants into small groups of three participants each and give each group a tangram puzzle. Tell them to keep the puzzle in the bag until you tell them to take it out.

2. When every group has a puzzle, explain that they will have ninety seconds to arrange the pieces into a rectangle, and that the first group to do so will win a prize. Tell them to take out their puzzles and begin.

3. When the first group finishes, if it is within the ninety seconds give the group a prize. Tell the other groups to continue until all groups have put their puzzles together.

4. Now ask the groups to mix up their puzzle pieces and, when you tell them to start, see whether they can arrange the pieces into a rectangle in sixty seconds. Again, give a prize to the first group finished within sixty seconds and let the other groups continue until they have put their puzzles together.

5. Next, ask the groups to mix up their puzzle pieces and explain that this time they are to arrange the pieces into some type of recognizable object or picture. Tell them they will have sixty seconds to do so.

6. When the sixty seconds are up, have them stop and take a look at each group's products. Let them guess what the objects or pictures are. Take digital pictures of all of their products. Let the group decide who gets the prize for the best arrangement.

7. Finally, have all the groups combine and pour all of their pieces together on a large table, or even on the floor if necessary. Tell them they will have five minutes to arrange the pieces into one picture or object using all of their pieces. Set a timer and place it where they can see it and hear it.

8. As they do this activity, take notes on how they carry out the activity. Look for leadership characteristics, effective team behaviors, roles that people take, and any other behaviors related to your program that will help you during the debriefing.

9. When the time is up, have the group explain their arrangement to you. Congratulate them on their "work of art" and distribute the large group prize. Take a picture of their final product.

10. Now debrief the activity using questions like these:

- What happened?

- What was easy and what was difficult?

- How did you agree on your final project?

- Who did what during the final project?

- What did you learn doing this activity?

PRICKLY POINTS

- Before you start this activity, ask how many participants are familiar with tangram puzzles. If many participants are familiar with them and have used them before, you will need to tighten your initial time limits. Instead of ninety seconds for the first activity and 60 for the second, you might want to make it sixty and forty-five seconds.

- The last activity works best on a table large enough for the group to all stand around it and work together.

- As soon as possible after the activity, print out copies of the products and post them on the wall.

VARIATIONS

- You can make the final activity more complicated and even include specifications if you like. For example, the specs might include: the final product can be no larger than nine inches by twelve inches; the final product must contain at least twenty-eight pieces, but no more than thirty-five pieces; only four people can work on the puzzle at the same time, but any number of substitutions of workers can occur at any time; and so forth. Try for specifications that imitate the workplace.

TEAM-BUILDING EXAMPLE

This is an excellent team-building activity. Use it to illustrate and analyze how the team works together. You can make the final activity as complicated or as simple as you like. A variation that I have used with teams is to give them plenty of time for the final activity, say ten minutes, and then three minutes into the activity, interrupt them and say that there has been a change in plans and upper management now says the project must be completed two minutes from now. This can lead to some interesting behaviors and a good debriefing.

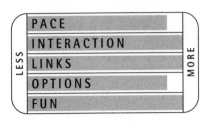

PACE	
INTERACTION	
LINKS	
OPTIONS	
FUN	

LESS — MORE

game 12.

A Stick by Any Other Name

Group Size: 9 to 30

Time Required: 30 to 45 minutes

Special Features: Link to your learners' creativity in this simple activity. It never ceases to amaze me how creative people can be when it comes to dreaming up uses for a bunch of plastic sticks.

Summary: In this imagination-stretching activity, participants start their creative juices flowing by coming up with a name, a use, and a slogan for a bunch of plastic sticks!

Goals: To serve as a warm-up activity and to stimulate creativity

Materials

- Flip chart paper and markers

- Six clear twelve-inch plastic sticks per small group (These can be found at hobby, craft, and sewing stores and are sometimes called quilting sticks.)

- A loud timer

- Masking tape or poster pins

- Prizes that can be shared

Physical Setting: Any space that will allow small groups of three to six participants to work on a creative project without being easily overheard by participants in other groups

● ●

PROCESS

1. Divide participants into small groups of three to six people per group and tell them to pretend that they are a creative design team working for Wonka Industries and that their boss, Wanda Wonka, has just sent them a memo. Read the following to them:

   Greetings Everyone!

   I just made the most amazing purchase. I can't believe how little I paid for these wonderful items. Nobody knows what these items are or what they can be used for, but who cares? With an incredibly creative team like you, whatever we decide to do with them, we're going to make a fortune! I'm sending a few of the items with this message so that you can begin. I want you to find a use for these items; give them a name; and write a slogan for them!

   Yours with high hopes,—Wanda

   p.s.—I bought a million of them!!

2. Tell the groups that you will soon be giving them a few of the objects that Wanda has discovered. Their assignment is to find a use for the items, give them a name, and write a slogan for them! They should then put all of this information on a flip chart that will be posted and shared with everyone.

3. Give each group a large sheet of flip chart paper and a few colored markers to record their final results to share with the rest of the group. Then send them to their assigned areas with instructions to return in ten minutes with the name, the use, and the slogan written on the flip chart page.

4. Pull out the plastic sticks and give each group a few. Set the timer and place it where it can be easily seen and heard.

5. When the timer goes off, have the participants reassemble. Ask them to keep their flip chart pages hidden until it is their group's time to share their ideas with the large group.

6. One-by-one, have a member from each group come to the front of the room, post their flip chart page on the wall, read it aloud, and explain it to the whole group.

7. After all flip chart pages have been posted, ask the group to determine which ideas should receive a prize. You might want to give prizes for "the most unusual use," "the most practical use," "the use that will make us the most money," or any others that you or the group come up with. Then distribute the prizes!

8. Debrief the activity using the following questions:

   • What happened when you began this activity?

   • How many ideas did you come up with?

   • How did you decide which idea you would use?

   • What was the most difficult part of this activity? Why?

● ●

PRICKLY POINTS

● Keep this activity light and fun.

● It's best to keep the plastic sticks out of sight until the moment they are required.

VARIATIONS

- Instead of flip charts and markers, assign the groups to produce a computer graphic that illustrates their results. They can project these onto a screen for viewing. This will require another ten minutes or more, but the results can be worth it.

TEAM-BUILDING EXAMPLE

This can be used as a warm-up activity before a creative-problem-solving session or just a fun energizer to start off a team meeting.

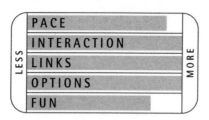

PACE	LESS				MORE
INTERACTION					
LINKS					
OPTIONS					
FUN					

Online Treasure Hunt

Group Size: Any size for which there are computers to access the Internet

Time Required: 45 minutes

Special Features: If you need a high-involvement activity that offers simultaneous choices and discovery learning, this is it.

Summary: Using a treasure hunt theme, participants go online to find the information needed to answer questions related to the training subject matter.

Goal: To acquaint participants with specific information related to the course

Materials

- List of items to be found on the treasure hunt

- One computer with online access for each participant or each small group of participants

- One large prize that can be shared—a treasure chest filled with goodies

- Many smaller prizes that can be shared, such as bags of chocolate medallions

Physical Setting: A classroom with computers that have Internet access

● ●

PROCESS

Before the Program

1. Prepare a list of ten to twenty questions related to the topic that you want participants to be aware of and that can be found on the company's intranet or on the Internet. For example, if you are teaching an orientation course, this could include information on company history, corporate initiatives, senior executives, HR policies and procedures, locations of various manufacturing plants or sales and service offices, and so forth. If you are teaching a customer service course, you might have them search for books on customer service, definitions of effective customer service, winners of awards given for effective customer service, and so on.

2. In preparing the list, try for a variety of difficulty. Make sure a few of the items are challenging and not easy to find. Also have a few funny or unusual items for participants to find.

3. Use a pirate or treasure-chest motif on the handout and have prizes that relate to the theme, such as chocolate coins, small treasure chests of jelly beans, and so forth.

During the Program

1. Divide the participants into small groups of three or four and tell them that they may work together in any way that they like. Say they will have twenty minutes to find the answers to questions on their list. Tell them that you will give a five-minute warning.

2. Say that the first group back with all of the right answers will win a "big" prize. Every other group that finds all the right answers within the time limit will also win a prize.

3. If some groups finish early, give them their prizes and ask them to use the remaining time to find other nifty items that could have been on your list!

4. When all groups have finished, go through the list and see what answers they have come up with. Have participants share where and how they found their information.

5. Debrief the activity with questions such as these:

   • What happened when you started looking for answers?

   • Which items were the easiest to find? Which were most difficult?

   • How will you use what you learned?

PRICKLY POINTS

   ● The time limit here can be tricky. You want there to be some time pressure, but you also want it to be possible for some participants to find the answers within the time limit. How long things take is also dependent on how many participants there are and how many computers they have access to.

   ● In general, the higher the number of participants with computer access, the less time will be needed. Sometimes I have given participants less time initially and then added another five or ten minutes if needed. This works pretty well.

VARIATIONS

   ● Depending on your topic, you might ask participants to find answers to questions and to find examples and illustrations of concepts that they will need to print out.

TEAM-BUILDING EXAMPLE

This activity can be used to have a team research a topic related to a team goal or problem. If the entire team finds all of the answers within the given time, then the whole team wins a prize that they can share.

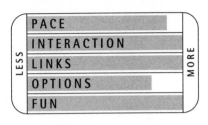

		LESS				MORE	
PACE							
INTERACTION							
LINKS							
OPTIONS							
FUN							

game 14

Generational Bingo

Group Size: 10 to 25 participants ranging in age from 25 to 55

Time Required: 30 to 45 minutes

Special Features: Link to your learners with this highly interactive game. It raises awareness of generational differences, and it's lots of fun as well.

Summary: Players mix and mingle in this bingo-style game, obtaining signatures from individuals who meet various generational descriptions on their bingo-style cards. Players win by obtaining signatures in either five boxes in a row, five in a column, or five diagonally across their cards.

Goals: To allow participants to meet one another and to raise awareness of generational differences

Materials

- Game cards for all participants

- Pencils or pens for writing on the cards

- Prizes

- Large, loud timer

Physical Setting: A large open area where players can easily mix and mingle

● ●

PROCESS

Before the Program

Print enough Generational Bingo cards for each player to have one using the form at the end of this activity. Print the cards on sturdy paper.

During the Program

1. Distribute the Generational Bingo cards and pens or pencils. Explain that each square on the card contains a description that could apply to various people in the group.

2. Explain how to play the game and go over the following rules:

   - In order to "cover" a square, a player must have that square signed or initialed by someone in the group who meets that description. For example, if the description says, "Watched the Beatles on 'The Ed Sullivan Show,'" then the player must find a person in the group who saw the Beatles on "The Ed Sullivan Show" and have that person sign that box.

   - A player can have his or her card signed only once by any individual in the group. For example, if I just signed your card for the descriptor "Studied Latin in high school," then I can't sign it again in any other box, even though I might be qualified for other box descriptors.

- Players should ask people directly and specifically about categories. In other words, do not ask, "Can you sign any of the squares on my card?" but, "Did you serve in Viet Nam?"

- Each player may only sign another player's card once. No player's name should appear more than once on a card.

- When any player has five squares signed across, down, or diagonally, he or she should take the card to the facilitator for a prize. There can be as many winners as time allows!

3. Have participants gather in a large open area. Tell them that they have ten minutes to mix and mingle and sign each other's cards. When anyone has a bingo, he or she should call out, "Bingo!" and come forward for a prize. Set the timer and place it where they can see it and hear it. There can be multiple winners.

4. When the timer goes off, ask the participants to return to their seats. Announce the winners and have the winners acknowledged by the group.

5. Conduct a debriefing using questions such as:

- What happened? Which categories did you look for first?

- Which categories did you hesitate to ask about? Why?

- Did you make any assumptions about other players?

- Did anyone make assumptions about you?

- Were there categories that you could have signed for but no one asked you?

- How age-diverse is this group? What effect does that have on our functioning?

PRICKLY POINTS

- Keep the play lively. Loudly announce it when someone gets a bingo.

- Points that you may also want to bring forth in the debriefing might be that it's easy to make assumptions about people, especially age-related assumptions, but that not all people from the same generation are alike. Also, point out that all generations have valuable knowledge and experience.

VARIATIONS

- If you run out of time and there have been no bingos, you might give the group another five minutes to keep trying or you could let players sign their own cards once.

- For a group of twelve or fewer, you can allow people to sign each other's cards twice to increase the chances of someone getting a bingo.

- For an interesting discussion of the generations, go over each of the twenty-five descriptors and discuss why each event had an impact on the generation that experienced it.

TEAM-BUILDING EXAMPLE

This is a good activity to use with a team that has members from different generations. It can be used to lead into a discussion of generational differences and how they affect the team.

Generational Bingo

Watched the Beatles on "The Ed Sullivan Show"	Uses a PDA	Had a car of his or her own while in high school	Waited in line to buy gas during OPEC embargo	Watched "Sesame Street" as a child
Can name the male lead on "Dawson's Creek"	Was in grade school in the seventies	Has played more than 500 hours of Nintendo	Remembers when Sputnik went up	Can name a day care center he or she attended
Can name three members of the Rat Pack	Studied Latin in high school	Uses a computer	First voted at the age of 18	Was in grade school in the fifties
Can name three members of the Brat Pack	Knows who Quentin Tarantino is	Has parents who are divorced	Turned 30 before AIDS was discovered	Has his or her own website
Used a computer by the age of 10	Served in Viet Nam or has a family member who did	Typed a copy using carbon paper	Used a cell phone before the age of 20	Listened to "The Lone Ranger" show on the radio

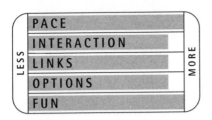

PACE
INTERACTION
LINKS
OPTIONS
FUN

LESS · MORE

Q&A Black Jack

Group Size: 8 to 24 participants

Time Required: 45 to 60 minutes

Special Features: This snappy card game is stimulating, tactile, and lots of fun.

Summary: Using a deck of question-and-answer cards, participants bet chips on knowing the answers to cards that are turned up by the Q&A dealer and continue until they lose all their chips or someone in their group accumulates twenty-five chips.

Goal: To increase general knowledge about the subject matter on the cards

Materials

- One deck of Q&A cards for every small group of four to six players

- One visor for each dealer, plus one for the instructor, and a whistle or horn for each dealer and the instructor

- Lots of white poker chips—enough for each player to start with ten white poker chips and each dealer to have one hundred chips

- Prizes that can be shared

- A horn for the instructor to blow

Physical Setting: Each group will need a table where the dealer can stand on one side and the players on the other

• •

PROCESS

Before the Program

1. Construct a deck of cards using either small index cards, cards cut from heavy paper, or blank playing cards that you have purchased from a teacher supply store. On each card put a specific question related to the subject matter of the training program and, on the other side, put the answer to the question. Make about half of the cards of medium difficulty and the other half of greater difficulty.

2. To help in sorting the cards, put a large Q on the question side and a large A on the answer side. You will need at least forty cards, more if possible. And you will need one card deck for every small group of four to six players.

3. Add two Jokers to every deck. You can make the Jokers look like some famous person or make Jokers that look like you.

During the Program

1. Divide the participants into small groups of four to six players and assign each group to a table. Ask the small groups to choose a dealer for their table and give each dealer a visor to wear during the activity.

2. Give each dealer a deck of Q&A cards and each table enough chips for all players at the table to receive ten white chips plus at least one hundred chips for the dealer.

3. Explain that when the play begins, the dealer will deal one card, question side up, in front of each player. Each player will have a different question card. Each player can bet one, two, or three chips on whether he or she will answer the question on the card correctly. Players have to bet at least one chip and can bet no more than three chips.

4. When all cards have been dealt and all players at the table have made their bets, the dealer will ask each player in turn the question on his or her card, and after each answer, the dealer will turn the card over to check the answer on the back.

5. If the answer is correct, the dealer will match the player's chips and the player will collect his or her winnings. If the answer is incorrect, the dealer will collect the chips and the player receives nothing. The dealer will collect all of the used cards and set them aside and deal fresh cards to all the players.

6. Once all question cards have been answered, the dealer will gather all of the cards, shuffle them, and use them again. The play continues for thirty minutes, until one player accumulates twenty-five chips, or until all players run out of chips! If two players accumulate twenty-five points in the same round, then that table has two winners.

7. Explain that each deck also contains two Jokers and that any time a Joker is turned up, the dealer will blow a horn and the instructor will bring a prize to the person who was dealt a Joker. The player with the Joker then has another card dealt to him or her and play continues.

8. The person at the table with the most chips at the end of the time limit, or the first person at the table to win twenty-five chips, or the only person at the table with any chips when the time is up is the winner at that table and receives a prize.

9. Once all tables have had a winner, hold a playoff round for the winners from each table. During this playoff round, have the dealer deal the cards after the players have made bets without knowing what the question is. In this final round players start with ten chips and the first player to acquire fifty chips wins the playoff.

10. Debrief with the following questions:

    • What happened when you began this activity?

    • How did you feel "betting" on your knowledge of the subject?

    • At what point did you begin to bet higher amounts?

    • What did you learn by doing this activity?

    • How can you apply what you learned?

PRICKLY POINTS

● Participants will sometimes become very involved with this game. Make sure all of your questions and answers are clear and correct. If someone disputes a question or answer, you can stop the play for a moment and let the group decide whether or not to keep the card in the deck or take it out.

● You can make the Joker prizes silly or edible or whatever you think will add to the fun of the game.

VARIATIONS

● The topics for this game can be almost anything—factual questions about a company product, about a country and a culture, about a computer program, about the company and its products, and so on.

● You can decide on how difficult you want the questions to be and perhaps even stack the decks according to some master training plan that you might have!

TEAM-BUILDING EXAMPLE

The card content can be anything that team members want or need to learn about, including special projects, new products or procedures, or team-development issues.

How to Construct Card Decks

- Prepare card content on a computer and print it out on card stock. Run one side through the printer for the questions and then the other side for the answers.

- Or you can prepare handwritten cards to be used.

- 8$\frac{1}{2}$-by-11-inch card stock can be cut easily into eight cards that are 4$\frac{1}{4}$ by 2$\frac{3}{4}$ inches.

- Many teacher supply stores carry blank cards that can be written on easily and work well.

- If nothing else, consider using 3-by-5-inch index cards.

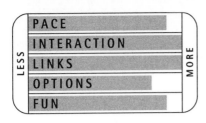

Approach and Coach

Group Size: 8 to 18

Time Required: 60 minutes

Special Features: Link to your learners by having them generate problem situations to work on and, while they do so, take digital pictures to use later.

Summary: Participants generate and discuss a number of performance improvement situations in terms of how someone could approach each person and coach him or her toward more productive behaviors.

Goals: To discuss a coaching situation and to practice using coaching behaviors

Materials

- Fifty blank note cards

- Pens or pencils

- Four baseball hats that say "Coach" and four that say "Super Coach"

- A flip chart and markers

- A digital camera, computer, and printer

- One small three-minute timer for each small group

- Prizes that can be shared

Physical Setting: Enough room for participants to sit in circles around tables in small groups of four or five

PROCESS

1. Ask participants to think of situations that they have encountered in the workplace where individuals were not performing well and could have benefited from a good coach. What situations have they been in where they themselves might have benefited from a performance coaching session?

2. Distribute blank note cards and pens or pencils and ask participants to write descriptions of at least two such situations on their cards.

3. While the groups are writing up situations, you can write the following on a flip chart for later use:

   • What performance needs to be improved?

   • How would you approach and coach in this situation?

   • What would you say?

4. When all participants have filled out cards, collect the cards and shuffle them into one big deck. Sort the participants into groups of four or five and have each group sit around a table. Divide the cards into as many stacks as there are groups and give each group a stack of cards. Ask them to spread the cards face up in the middle of the table.

5. Hand one person in each group a hat that says "Coach." Explain that, one by one, starting with the person who received (and is hopefully wearing) the coaching hat, people will choose a card, discuss the situation on the card by answering the questions on the flip chart, and then demonstrate what they would say if they were to coach the person in the situation described on the card.

6. To keep things moving quickly, give each group a three-minute timer and tell them to use the timers for the discussion. When three minutes are up, it is time for the "coach" in each group to demonstrate what he or she would say if asked to coach the person in the situation.

7. When each "coach" finishes with the card that he or she has chosen, he or she should pass the "Coach" hat to the person on his or her left, who then chooses another card and follows the same process. This continues until all of the cards have been discussed.

8. Finally, have each small group choose the two "most difficult" cards from the stack and turn them in to you. They should also choose someone from their group to be "Super Coach" in a final all-groups round.

9. While the activity is going on, take digital pictures of the participants wearing the hats and interacting in their groups.

10. Have participants return to their regular seats. For the final round, spread the "most difficult" cards on a table at the front and have the "Super Coaches" come forward. One-by-one, ask the Super Coaches to choose a card, read the card out loud, and respond as if they were coaching that person. Be sure to take a picture of each Super Coach.

11. Award each Super Coach a prize when they are finished.

12. Debrief the activity with questions such as these:

    • Who has the right to approach and coach someone?

    • Who do you have the most difficulty approaching and coaching?

    • Have you ever known a "Super Coach"? What was he or she like?

13. Print and post pictures from this activity and give copies to people at the end of the program.

PRICKLY POINTS

- It helps if you can start things with a good role model, so initially give the coaching hats to participants you think will do well in this activity.

- Pause a moment before you take anyone's picture and allow people the chance to say no. Not everyone likes to see him- or herself in a baseball hat.

VARIATIONS

- This activity can be used in a variety of classes with the coach coaching whatever behaviors are being studied, for example, the Customer Service Coach, the Quality Coach, and so forth.

TEAM-BUILDING EXAMPLE

The Team-Building Coach can coach for certain targeted team behaviors, such as cooperation, encouragement, and so on.

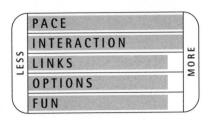

	PACE	
	INTERACTION	
LESS	LINKS	MORE
	OPTIONS	
	FUN	

Ready, Set, Goal

Group Size: 6 to 24

Time Required: 90 minutes

Special Features: Keep things snappy and get participants interacting with this hands-on, learn-by-doing, skill-building activity.

Summary: Instead of talking about goal setting, this fast-paced flip chart activity has participants working in small groups actually doing four rounds of goal setting.

Goal: To practice basic goal-setting skills

Materials

- Enlarged copies of the goal-setting model to fit onto flip charts or to hang on the walls

- One flip chart and markers for each small group

- Handouts with the goal-setting model and information on goal setting

- A whistle

- Lots of prizes that can be shared by small groups

- Masking tape or push pins

Physical Setting: Enough space for small groups to form around flip charts placed throughout the room

• •

PROCESS

Before the Program

1. Make large copies of the goal-setting model on page 160 and post them four to a flip chart on flip charts set out around the room.

2. Make a regular-sized copy of the goal-setting handout for each participant.

During the Program

1. Divide the participants into groups of three or four people and send each group to a flip chart. Have them look over the goal-setting chart on their flip chart as you distribute the handout. Tell them that the handout gives the goal-setting procedure that they will be following and that they can refer to it as needed.

2. Explain to the group that they will first be filling out a goal-setting chart on how to lose ten pounds in five weeks. Have them write that as their goal on the line following the word "goal": *lose ten pounds in five weeks.*

3. Next ask them to generate three objectives that, if achieved, would help them meet their goal (for example, eat less, exercise more, keep motivated, and so forth). Have the groups compare and discuss their objectives. Ask them if their objectives, if achieved, would help them meet their goal.

4. Now tell the groups they have five minutes to generate realistic actions for each objective and that, when the time is up, you will blow a whistle and the group with the most actions listed will receive a prize. After five minutes blow the whistle, ask them to stop, and then have them compare and discuss their actions. Are the actions realistic? Award a prize to the group with the most actions listed.

5. Ask the participants to number off within their groups and then ask participants who are number one to leave the group they are in and move on to the nearest group to their right.

6. When participants have done this, have them turn to a fresh goal-setting page on their flip charts. Tell the groups that they are going to do another practice activity, this time using the goal *Learn conversational Japanese in three months*. Give them ten minutes to accomplish this task by writing appropriate objectives and actions.

7. After the ten minutes are up, blow the whistle and have groups share and compare their goals and activities. Let them determine the group that receives a prize and give a prize to the group they chose.

8. Do a mini-debriefing by asking:

    • What makes a good goal? What makes good objectives?

    • How realistic are your activities?

    • Did you put anything down as an activity that you know you wouldn't really do?

9. Next have all the participants generate a number of problems to be addressed in the workplace in general or within their own workgroups and jobs specifically. Post a list of these problems on a wall where all can see.

10. Remind them that last time when they numbered off, participants numbered one had to go to a different group. Now ask that all participants who earlier had the number two to leave the groups they are in and go to the next group to their left.

11. Now ask each group to choose a problem from the list, and say that they will have fifteen minutes to generate a goal, objectives, and activities to address their chosen problem. When each group has chosen a problem, blow the whistle and tell them to "Begin!"

12. When time is up, blow the whistle and ask the groups to stop. Let the groups present and critique their products to each other, and let them determine the group that receives a prize.

13. Now say that it is time for the participants who are number three to leave their present groups and move on to the next group to their right.

14. As a final round, let the groups pick any topic from the list, and this time give them only ten minutes. Again let them debrief by themselves and let them award themselves prizes for categories like "the most innovative activity," "the most ambitious plan," and "the most un-doable activity."

15. Do a final debriefing using questions such as these:

   • What happened as you did more rounds of this activity?

   • Did it become easier to follow the model?

   • Which part of the model is most difficult?

   • What did you learn about goal setting?

   • How will you use what you learned?

PRICKLY POINTS

● This activity is most effective when done briskly and matter-of-factly, but with a good sense of humor. As the groups are sharing and comparing their goals, objectives, and activities, give them lots of feedback and reinforcement.

● Point out particularly good actions. Elicit suggestions for making actions even better, that is, more specific, measurable, or whatever.

VARIATIONS

● If time is limited you can always eliminate one of the four rounds.

● Instead of printing up large copies of the goal-setting chart, you can give each group a small chart and let them use it as a guide for writing on their flip chart pages.

TEAM-BUILDING EXAMPLE

Use this activity as a team goal-setting vehicle, and let the team decide on problems they need to address and then address them. Large teams can divide into smaller groups with each group taking a different problem and then sharing their results with the whole team.

Goal: _____

_____

_____

Objective 1

_____

_____

Objective 2

_____

_____

Objective 3

_____

_____

Activities for Objective 1

_____

_____

_____

_____

_____

_____

_____

_____

_____

_____

_____

_____

_____

_____

_____

_____

Activities for Objective 2

_____

_____

_____

_____

_____

_____

_____

_____

_____

_____

_____

_____

_____

_____

_____

_____

Activities for Objective 3

_____

_____

_____

_____

_____

_____

_____

_____

_____

_____

_____

_____

_____

_____

_____

_____

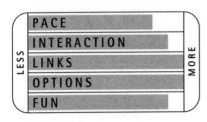

PACE	
INTERACTION	
LINKS	
OPTIONS	
FUN	

LESS   MORE

game **18**

Involve to Solve

Group Size: 6 to 30

Time Required: 2 hours

Special Features: This self-directed, small-group research activity allows participants to investigate a problem of their choice and generate ideas on how to address the problem.

Summary: Participants are given a problem to investigate, guidelines to follow in their investigation, and a report-back time to share their findings.

Goals: To gather information and to stimulate problem solving on a particular topic.

Materials

- Copies of an issue handout

- Computers with online access

- Flip charts and markers

- Digital projection capabilities

- Prizes that can be shared

Physical Setting: Classroom with computers with online access

● ●

PROCESS

Before the Program

1. Choose a major issue for this activity and develop a handout that states the major issue and then lists a few problems related to the issue. Have the problems stated in question form, such as "How can we increase (decrease, improve, etc.) X?" Have copies of this handout and activity guidelines ready to distribute to the class.

2. Consider using a detective theme for this activity. Have each group give themselves a name and use that name and theme in their final presentation.

During the Program

1. Distribute the handout and go over it with the participants. Tell them that their assignment is to choose a problem, research it, and come up with suggestions on how to address (and perhaps even solve) that problem.

2. Ask the participants for any additional problems to be added to the list and then have them add any that come up.

3. Ask the participants to form groups of four to six people and tell them that after they choose their problem, they may use the following approaches to research that problem:

   - Find out what others elsewhere are doing to address this problem

   - Brainstorm ideas, choose a few, and develop them

   - Survey those involved with the problem to come up with ideas

   - Use a mix of the above

4. In terms of resources, set these guidelines:

   - Contact anyone you like as long as you do not significantly disrupt that person's work

   - Use online sources and resources

   - Use any written resources within this building

5. Tell the groups that they can do their research any way they like and then work together as a group to analyze their findings and come up with recommendations. They should then work together to prepare a five- to ten-minute presentation of their findings and recommendations to give to the entire group. Presentations should be high-tech, high fun, and highly informative.

6. Explain that you will award various prizes after their presentations, including awards for the most thorough research, the most creative solutions, the most effective presentation of findings, and so forth.

7. Tell them what time presentations will begin, say that you will be happy to help them any way that you can (within reason), and tell them to begin.

8. When it is time, have all groups make their presentations and then present the prizes.

9. Debrief the content of the presentations using questions such as:

   - What common themes and ideas did you notice in your presentations?

   - What seem to be the most practical ideas? The least expensive ideas?

   - What ideas do you think would be most effective? Why?

· ·

PRICKLY POINTS

- For this activity to be effective, the research topics must be interesting and meaningful to the participants. Obtain their input before they begin their projects and make sure they are interested in their chosen problem.

- Encourage the groups to stretch themselves and go for new and unusual ideas and information.

VARIATIONS

- This activity can be used as an assignment between training sessions.

- Use it as pre-work before a training class.

TEAM–BUILDING EXAMPLE

This activity can be used as an assignment between team meetings or as an ongoing project for a team.

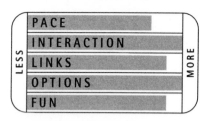
PACE		
INTERACTION		
LINKS		
OPTIONS		
FUN		

LESS · MORE

Across the Board

Group Size: 8 to 16

Time Required: 2 hours

Special Features: Participants are faced with lots of options and choices as they design their own board games.

> **Summary:**   This review activity has two groups of participants design board games to test the material in their assigned topic. They then exchange games and try them out.

Goal: To review important course content

Materials

● Two boxes filled with materials for constructing board games

- Poster boards, construction paper, and colored markers

- Copies of The Basics of Board Game Design (page 168)

- Prizes that can be easily shared

Physical Setting: Breakout rooms or two large tables in the classroom

● ●

PROCESS

Before the Program

1. Put together two boxes of materials for constructing board games. Each box should contain colored markers, dice, a spinner, pawns, three or four undecorated game boards, decks of blank cards, and a variety of stickers (castles, kings, monsters, magicians, detectives, sports equipment, and so forth).

2. Put in a few unusual and fun items like paste and glitter, a few weird objects that can be used as pawns, and so on.

During the Program

1. Explain to the participants that, as a review of important class content, they will be designing board games that test information related to the major topics that have been covered in the class.

2. Divide the participants into two groups and assign each group to a breakout room or an area of the classroom that they may use to design their games.

3. Assign the groups different topics that have been covered in the class. Give each group a box of materials for constructing their board games and copies of the handout. Tell them they will have forty-five minutes in which to design and construct their games. Give them a time by which they should return to the classroom with their completed games.

4. When the time is up, have participants return to the main room and let each group make a short presentation of their game and how it works.

5. After the presentations, tell the groups to switch and play the other game. Tell them the first winner at each game board will receive a prize.

6. When each game has had at least one winner, stop the game play and award prizes.

7. Debrief with these questions:

   • What happened?

   • What was it like having to design a board game?

   • What was easy and what was difficult?

   • What did you learn?

PRICKLY POINTS

   ● Choose just the key topics to be covered in the games.

   ● Be sure the two teams are not working on any of the same material.

VARIATIONS

   ● This game can also be used as a primary vehicle to cover almost any course material. As a primary teaching tool, it is better to have the two groups working on the same material. That way they have a double opportunity to learn.

TEAM–BUILDING EXAMPLE

The team can do this activity focusing on key information that will be helpful to the team. Divide the team into two groups and let them work on different aspects of the topic and then exchange games.

The Basics of Board Game Design

1. **Decide on the type of cards you want to use.** Choose from one of the following:

   Fact or data cards. These contain questions about the subject matter.

   Multiple-choice questions. Each of these cards has a question with four possible answers on it. The question, the choices, and the answer are all on the front of the card. With this type of card, the opponent draws the card and quizzes the player.

2. **Create a deck of cards.** This is a major element of creating a board game. There must be a fairly large number of cards. If you will have four people or fewer playing and it will take each person at least five and possibly eight rolls of the dice before someone reaches the finish line, then you will need at least thirty cards and maybe forty or more to be safe.

3. **Decide on the look and theme of the game board.** Consider a simple pathway around the perimeter of the board. Or try a figure-eight design. Or you might want to try a round pathway with crossing pathways across the diameter of the circle. Decide on how many spaces you want around the board. If the most any one player can roll on any one turn is a six, and you want each player to have at least four turns, then you will need at least thirty spaces. Design your game board on construction paper, $8\frac{1}{2}$ by 11 or $8\frac{1}{2}$ by 14. Consider taping two sheets of paper together to create an even larger game board.

4. **Decide how to determine forward movement.** Dice can be used or a spinner. I have found the use of a single die most effective for small game boards that accommodate two to four players. Fewer spaces are needed, and it's just easier to use the one die.

5. **Determine the basic procedure of the game.**

   • Decide how the game will be played. Each player needs an object to move around the board. This can be a coin, a plastic pawn, or even a foil-wrapped chocolate!

   • What does a player do when it is his or her turn? Draw a card and answer the question on it? Or does the other team draw the card and ask the question? If the player answers correctly, does he or she move ahead the number of spaces on the die? Or does the player roll the die and move ahead that many spaces, then draw a card and discuss it with the group?

- Or the cards could have numbers on them and you wouldn't need dice. A player could draw a card, answer the question on the card, and move that many spaces ahead. You could determine the number of spaces to move forward by the difficulty of the question on the card, that is, the harder the question the more spaces forward.

6. **Put it all together and try it out.**

- Write out directions for the board game. Include rules, regulations, and what it takes to win.

- Use a couple of coins for moving objects, get a die, set the card deck next to the game board, and try things out. See how long it takes to get around the board.

- Imagine or act out three or four people playing the game, drawing cards, discussing answers, moving the game pieces around the board. How long do you estimate the game will take?

	LESS		MORE
PACE			
INTERACTION			
LINKS			
OPTIONS			
FUN			

Jelly Bean Art

Group Size: 6 to 18

Time Required: 20 minutes

Special Features: Why not go out with a bang as well as start with one? This closing activity is quick, easy, fun, and lets the learners express themselves.

Summary: As a closing activity, participants use jelly beans to draw a picture of what they liked best about the class.

Goals: To let participants review class content and to enjoy a final fun activity

Materials

- Large paper plates or square aluminum trays

- Large bags of multicolored jelly beans

- One small bag of jelly beans for each participant

Physical Setting: Tables for participants to work on the jelly bean projects

● ●

Process

1. Put the participants into small groups of five to six people and give each group a large paper plate or tray, a large bag of jelly beans, and instructions to arrange the jelly beans on the paper plate in a way that illustrates something that they liked best about the class.

2. Give them ten minutes to accomplish this. Set a timer and place it where the participants can see it and hear it.

3. When the timer goes off, let the groups look at the various "artworks" and see whether they can guess what is depicted in the jelly bean art.

4. Thank them for their contributions throughout the day and for their lovely artwork. Then give each participant his or her own little bag of jelly beans.

● ●

Prickly Points

● It helps to use fairly large bags of jelly beans and to have a couple of extra bags that you keep with you. I've done this activity so many times when a desperate representative from one of the groups rushes to my side begging for more green jelly beans. Remember, art has not only a mind of its own, but a need for endless jelly beans.

● ●

Variations

● You can change what you ask the jelly bean art to portray. Ask for the most important thing participants learned, what they are going to do differently after they leave, or whatever seems appropriate for your program.

- Instead of jelly beans you could use M&M®s, Hershey's Kisses® in different colored wrappers, or even colored macaroni.

Team-Building Example

This is always a nice closing activity for a team-building class or even a team meeting.

References

Barker, J. (1985). *Discovering the future: The business of paradigms.* St. Paul, MN: ILI Press.

Davis, S. (1987). *Future perfect.* Reading, MA: Addison-Wesley.

Dychtwald, K. (1999). *Age power: How the 21st century will be ruled by the new old.* New York: Tarcher/Putnam.

Goode, E. (2000, August 8). How culture molds habits of thought. *The New York Times,* p. 1, Section F.

Holtz, G. (1995). *Welcome to the jungle: The why behind generation X.* New York: St. Martin's Griffin.

Howe, N., & Strauss, W. (2000). *Millennials rising: The next great generations.* New York: Vintage Books.

Interactive Digital Software Association. (2003). Available: www.idsa.com/pressroom.html.

Jones, S. (2003). *Let the games begin.* Washington, DC: PEW Research Center. (www.pewinternet.org)

Knowles, M. (1998). *The adult learner.* Houston, TX: Gulf.

North Central Regional Educational Laboratory. (2002). www.ncrel.org.

Prensky, M. (2001). *Digital game-based learning.* New York: McGraw-Hill.

Rasenberger, J. (2000, March). *My generation sucks.* Available: www.salon.com/people/feature/2000/03/01/genvy/html

Salopek, J. (2000). The young and the rest of us: Should trainers tailor their techniques depending on the age of the audience? *Training & Development, 54*(2), 26–30.

Tapscott, D. (1998). *Growing up digital: The rise of the net generation.* New York: McGraw-Hill.

Zemke, R., Raines, C., & Filipczak, B. (2000). *Generations at work: Managing the clash of veterans, boomers, Xers, and nexters in your workplace.* New York: American Management Association.

Appendix

Survey Results

In my research regarding the design and delivery of training for younger learners, I found people like Mark Prensky, Don Tapscott, and others writing about the need for speed, connectivity, and interaction in younger learners. They also wrote of the capacity of younger learners to randomly access and parallel process a variety of information simultaneously, the need for more customized learning, and an expectation or need for learning to be fun.

What they wrote certainly seemed to correspond to what I had observed in my training programs over the past few years and to what I saw and heard in my interactions with learners from the younger generations. However, I wanted to get some concrete comments and feedback about these issues from the learners themselves. My intention was not to conduct "official" or "in-depth" research, but to obtain a personal sense of what younger learners think about these issues.

I decided to assess the opinions of younger learners regarding these factors through a simple survey where they could respond to twenty statements on a five-point scale. I used a variety of statements covering the factors mentioned above and asked respondents to rate these aspects of training and educational programs as very important, important, somewhat important, not very important, or not important at all. The surveys were given to seventy university undergraduate and graduate students between the ages of nineteen and thirty-nine. Their responses are shown on the following pages.

The survey was followed by a few open-ended questions about their ideal educational class or seminar, the ideal qualities of an instructor, and what they dislike the most in training and educational programs. Their responses to the open-ended questions are given throughout the book.

Survey Results*

The following scale was used for the survey.

4 = very important
3 = important
2 = somewhat important
1 = not very important
0 = not important at all

	4	3	2	1	0
1. Start the program with a bang! I don't like to sit and wait forever for something to happen.	25	31	9	5	0
2. Use a variety of materials and media that appeal to all the senses. I like to see it, hear it, and get my hands on it.	40	23	5	2	0
3. Have each participant stand and tell the group a little bit about him- or herself so that we can all get better acquainted.	4	5	25	23	13
4. Have different activities occurring at the same time and let the learners go back and forth and in and out of activities as they like.	5	15	35	8	7
5. Include activities where we can solve problems using information and techniques that we are learning in the training.	22	33	13	1	0
6. Avoid fun, fantasy, and imaginary elements as much as possible.	10	6	8	24	22
7. Maintain a nice, calm, easy pace throughout the workshop.	11	22	22	11	2
8. Have lots of involving activities and games that make learning fun.	32	25	10	2	1

*Seventy respondents ranged from ages 19 to 39.

	4	3	2	1	0
9. Have illustrations and examples that are relevant to my age and my interests.	38	23	7	2	0
10. Intersperse the day with a variety of rewards and incentives.	17	22	19	9	3
11. Keep the use of technology to a minimum. Use mostly printed materials.	1	2	10	32	25
12. Offer options and choices whenever possible. Let the learners pick what they want to do sometimes and decide how they want to do it.	10	30	26	3	1
13. Keep a fast overall tempo to the day. Move through the material quickly and energetically.	12	19	20	16	3
14. Use a lot of lecturing. Tell us what you want us to know. Give us lots of printed information.	1	5	8	27	29
15. Provide activities in which we can discover basic principles and apply new concepts. Let us learn by doing.	18	38	11	2	1
16. Make use of fantasy themes and imaginary settings in some of the games and activities.	11	22	21	13	3
17. Try to keep things sequential; use a step-by-step approach. Have everyone do the same thing at the same time.	8	15	24	16	7
18. Make use of different technologies throughout the training. Let participants use technology as part of the learning.	21	26	16	5	2
19. Conduct the program in a quiet, calm, relaxing way, especially at the beginning.	2	6	31	17	14
20. Keep fun and games to a minimum. Learning is serious business.	0	4	6	18	42

The six most important items chosen by 70 respondents are as follows:

1. Use a variety of materials and media that appeal to all the senses. I like to see it, hear it, and get my hands on it.

2. Have illustrations and examples that are relevant to my age and my interests.

3. Have lots of involving activities and games that make the learning fun.

4. Start the program with a bang! I don't like to sit and wait forever for something to happen.

5. Provide activities in which we can discover basic principles and apply new concepts. Let us learn by doing.

6. Include activities where we can solve problems using information and techniques that we are learning in the training.

The three least important items chosen (the three things most important not to do):

1. Keep fun and games to a minimum. Learning is serious business.

2. Keep the use of technology to a minimum. Use mostly printed materials.

3. Use a lot of lecturing. Tell us what you want us to know. Give us lots of printed information.

About the Author

Dr. Susan El-Shamy is senior partner at Advancement Strategies, Inc., a training and development resources company in Bloomington, IN, where she utilizes her extensive training experience in the research, design, and delivery of Advancement Strategies' training products and programs. For almost twenty years, Dr. El-Shamy has delivered training programs nationally and internationally for a variety of companies, including Berlitz, Corning, GMAC, Mattel, Motorola, Prudential, and Thomson Consumer Electronics. She is a regular guest lecturer at the Indiana University School of Business and a frequent speaker at national training conferences.

Her publications include:

- *Dynamic Induction: Games, Activities, and Ideas to Revitalize Your Employee Orientation Process* (London: Gower, 2003);

- *Training Games: Everything You Need to Know About Using Games to Reinforce Learning* (Stylus Publications, 2001);

- *Card Games for Developing Service* (London: Gower, 2001);

- *Card Games for Developing Teams* (London: Gower and Amherst, MA: HRD Press, 2000);

- *Action Pack Learning Cards* (Bloomington, IN: Advancement Strategies, Inc., 1995–1997); and

- *Diversity Bingo: An Experiential Learning Activity* (San Francisco: Pfeiffer, 1994).

Dr. El-Shamy has a bachelor's degree in radio and television, a master's degree in English, and a doctor of education degree in counseling and guidance. She has worked in higher education in a number of capacities, including assistant dean of students at Indiana University and associate dean of students at the American University in Cairo, Egypt.

How to Use the CD-ROM

SYSTEM REQUIREMENTS

WINDOWS PC

- 486 or Pentium processor-based personal computer

- Microsoft Windows 95 or Windows NT 3.51 or later

- Minimum RAM: 8MB for Windows 95 and NT

- Available space on hard disk: 8 MB Windows 95 and NT

- 2X speed CD-ROM drive or faster

MACINTOSH

- Macintosh with a 68020 or higher processor or Power Macintosh

- Apple OS version 7.0 or later

- Minimum RAM: 12MB for Macintosh

- Available space on hard disk: 6MB Macintosh

- 2X speed CD-ROM drive or faster

NOTE: This CD-ROM requires Netscape 3.0 or MS Internet Explorer 3.0 or higher.

GETTING STARTED

Insert the CD-ROM into your drive. The CD-ROM will usually launch automatically. If it does not, click on the CD-ROM drive on your computer to launch. After you click to agree to the terms of the Copyright Page, the Home Page will appear.

MOVING AROUND

Use the buttons at the left of each screen to move among the menu pages. To view a document listed on one of the menu pages, simply click on the name of the document. To quit a document at any time, click the box at the upper right-hand corner of the screen.

To quit the CD-ROM, you can click the Exit button or hit Alt-F4.

TO DOWNLOAD DOCUMENTS

Open the document you wish to download. Under the File pulldown menu, choose Save As. Save the document onto your hard drive with a different name. It is important to use a different name, otherwise the document may remain a read-only file.

You can also click on your CD drive in Windows Explorer and select a document to copy it to your hard drive and rename it.

IN CASE OF TROUBLE

If you experience difficulty using this CD-ROM, please follow these steps:

1. Make sure your hardware and systems configurations conform to the systems requirements noted under "Systems Requirements" above.

2. Review the installation procedure for your type of hardware and operating system. It is possible to reinstall the software if necessary.

3. Have a question, comment, or suggestion? Contact us! We value your feedback, and we want to hear from you.

For questions about this or other Pfeiffer products, you may contact us by:

E-mail: customer@wiley.com

Mail: Customer Care Wiley/Pfeiffer
             10475 Crosspoint Blvd.
             Indianapolis, IN 46256

Phone: (U.S.) 800-274-4434   (Outside the U.S. 317-572-3985)

Fax: (U.S.) 800-569-0443   (Outside the U.S. 317-572-4002)

To order additional copies of this product or to browse other Pfeiffer products visit us online at www.pfeiffer.com.

To speak with someone in Product Technical Support, call 800-762-2974 or 317-572-3994 Monday through Friday 8:30 A.M. to 5 P.M. (EST). You can also contact Product Technical Support and get support information through our website at http://www.wiley.com/tech-support

Before calling or writing, please have the following information available:

*   Type of operating system

*   Any error messages displayed

*   Complete description of the problem

It is best if you are sitting at your computer when making the call.

Pfeiffer Publications Guide

This guide is designed to familiarize you with the various types of Pfeiffer publications. The formats section describes the various types of products that we publish; the methodologies section describes the many different ways that content might be provided within a product. We also provide a list of the topic areas in which we publish.

FORMATS

In addition to its extensive book-publishing program, Pfeiffer offers content in an array of formats, from field-books for the practitioner to complete, ready-to-use training packages that support group learning.

FIELDBOOK Designed to provide information and guidance to practitioners in the midst of action. Most field-books are companions to another, sometimes earlier, work, from which its ideas are derived; the fieldbook makes practical what was theoretical in the original text. Fieldbooks can certainly be read from cover to cover. More likely, though, you'll find yourself bouncing around following a particular theme, or dipping in as the mood, and the situation, dictate.

HANDBOOK A contributed volume of work on a single topic, comprising an eclectic mix of ideas, case studies, and best practices sourced by practitioners and experts in the field.

An editor or team of editors usually is appointed to seek out contributors and to evaluate content for relevance to the topic. Think of a handbook not as a ready-to-eat meal, but as a cookbook of ingredients that enables you to create the most fitting experience for the occasion.

RESOURCE Materials designed to support group learning. They come in many forms: a complete, ready-to-use exercise (such as a game); a comprehensive resource on one topic (such as conflict management) containing a variety of methods and approaches; or a collection of like-minded activities (such as icebreakers) on multiple subjects and situations.

TRAINING PACKAGE An entire, ready-to-use learning program that focuses on a particular topic or skill. All packages comprise a guide for the facilitator/trainer and a workbook for the participants. Some packages are supported with additional media—such as video—or learning aids, instruments, or other devices to help participants understand concepts or practice and develop skills.

- *Facilitator/trainer's guide* Contains an introduction to the program, advice on how to organize and facilitate the learning event, and step-by-step instructor notes. The guide also contains copies of presentation materials—handouts, presentations, and overhead designs, for example—used in the program.

- *Participant's workbook* Contains exercises and reading materials that support the learning goal and serves as a valuable reference and support guide for participants in the weeks and months that follow the learning event. Typically, each participant will require his or her own workbook.

ELECTRONIC CD-ROMs and web-based products transform static Pfeiffer content into dynamic, interactive experiences. Designed to take advantage of the searchability, automation, and ease-of-use that technology provides, our e-products bring convenience and immediate accessibility to your workspace.

METHODOLOGIES

CASE STUDY A presentation, in narrative form, of an actual event that has occurred inside an organization. Case studies are not prescriptive, nor are they used to prove a point; they are designed to develop critical analysis and decision-making skills. A case study has a specific time frame, specifies a sequence of events, is narrative in structure, and contains a plot structure—an issue (what should be/have been done?). Use case studies when the goal is to enable participants to apply previously learned theories to the circumstances in the case, decide what is pertinent, identify the real issues, decide what should have been done, and develop a plan of action.

ENERGIZER A short activity that develops readiness for the next session or learning event. Energizers are most commonly used after a break or lunch to stimulate or refocus the group. Many involve some form of physical activity, so they are a useful way to counter post-lunch lethargy. Other uses include transitioning from one topic to another, where "mental" distancing is important.

EXPERIENTIAL LEARNING ACTIVITY (ELA) A facilitator-led intervention that moves participants through the learning cycle from experience to application (also known as a Structured Experience). ELAs are carefully thought-out designs in which there is a definite learning purpose and intended outcome. Each step—everything that participants do during the activity—facilitates the accomplishment of the stated goal. Each ELA includes complete instructions for facilitating the intervention and a clear statement of goals, suggested group size and timing, materials required, an explanation of the process, and, where appropriate, possible variations to the activity. (For more detail on Experiential Learning Activities, see the Introduction to the *Reference Guide to Handbooks and Annuals*, 1999 edition, Pfeiffer, San Francisco.)

GAME A group activity that has the purpose of fostering team spirit and togetherness in addition to the achievement of a pre-stated goal. Usually contrived—undertaking a desert expedition, for example—this type of learning method offers an engaging means for participants to demonstrate and practice business and interpersonal skills. Games are effective for team building and personal development mainly because the goal is subordinate to the process—the means through which participants reach decisions, collaborate, communicate, and generate trust and understanding. Games often engage teams in "friendly" competition.

ICEBREAKER A (usually) short activity designed to help participants overcome initial anxiety in a training session and/or to acquaint the participants with one another. An icebreaker can be a fun activity or can be tied to specific topics or training goals. While a useful tool in itself, the icebreaker comes into its own in situations where tension or resistance exists within a group.

INSTRUMENT A device used to assess, appraise, evaluate, describe, classify, and summarize various aspects of human behavior. The term used to describe an instrument depends primarily on its format and purpose. These terms include survey, questionnaire, inventory, diagnostic, survey, and poll. Some uses of instruments include providing instrumental feedback to group members, studying here-and-now processes or functioning within a group, manipulating group composition, and evaluating outcomes of training and other interventions.

Instruments are popular in the training and HR field because, in general, more growth can occur if an individual is provided with a method for focusing specifically on his or her own behavior. Instruments also are used to obtain information that will serve as a basis for change and to assist in workforce planning efforts.

Paper-and-pencil tests still dominate the instrument landscape with a typical package comprising a facilitator's guide, which offers advice on administering the instrument and interpreting the collected data, and an initial set of instruments. Additional instruments are available separately. Pfeiffer, though, is investing heavily in e-instruments. Electronic instrumentation provides effortless distribution and, for larger groups particularly, offers advantages over paper-and-pencil tests in the time it takes to analyze data and provide feedback.

LECTURETTE A short talk that provides an explanation of a principle, model, or process that is pertinent to the participants' current learning needs. A lecturette is intended to establish a common language bond between the trainer and the participants by providing a mutual frame of reference. Use a lecturette as an introduction to a group activity or event, as an interjection during an event, or as a handout.

MODEL A graphic depiction of a system or process and the relationship among its elements. Models provide a frame of reference and something more tangible, and more easily remembered, than a verbal explanation. They also give participants something to "go on," enabling them to track their own progress as they experience the dynamics, processes, and relationships being depicted in the model.

ROLE PLAY A technique in which people assume a role in a situation/scenario: a customer service rep in an angry-customer exchange, for example. The way in which the role is approached is then discussed and feedback is offered. The role play is often repeated using a different approach and/or incorporating changes made based on feedback received. In other words, role playing is a spontaneous interaction involving realistic behavior under artificial (and safe) conditions.

SIMULATION A methodology for understanding the interrelationships among components of a system or process. Simulations differ from games in that they test or use a model that depicts or mirrors some aspect of reality in form, if not necessarily in content. Learning occurs by studying the effects of change on one or more factors of the model. Simulations are commonly used to test hypotheses about what happens in a system—often referred to as "what if?" analysis—or to examine best-case/worst-case scenarios.

THEORY A presentation of an idea from a conjectural perspective. Theories are useful because they encourage us to examine behavior and phenomena through a different lens.

TOPICS

The twin goals of providing effective and practical solutions for workforce training and organization development and meeting the educational needs of training and human resource professionals shape Pfeiffer's publishing program. Core topics include the following:

Leadership & Management

Communication & Presentation

Coaching & Mentoring

Training & Development

E-Learning

Teams & Collaboration

OD & Strategic Planning

Human Resources

Consulting

What will you find on pfeiffer.com?

- The best in workplace performance solutions for training and HR professionals

- Downloadable training tools, exercises, and content

- Web-exclusive offers

- Training tips, articles, and news

- Seamless on-line ordering

- Author guidelines, information on becoming a Pfeiffer Affiliate, and much more

Discover more at www.pfeiffer.com

Customer Care

Have a question, comment, or suggestion? Contact us! We value your feedback and we want to hear from you.

For questions about this or other Pfeiffer products, you may contact us by:

E-mail: **customer@wiley.com**

Mail: **Customer Care Wiley/Pfeiffer**
10475 Crosspoint Blvd.
Indianapolis, IN 46256

Phone: **(US) 800-274-4434** (Outside the US: 317-572-3985)

Fax: **(US) 800-569-0443** (Outside the US: 317-572-4002)

To order additional copies of this title or to browse other Pfeiffer products, visit us online at **www.pfeiffer.com**.

For **Technical Support** questions call **(800) 274-4434.**

For authors guidelines, log on to www.pfeiffer.com and click on "Resources for Authors."

If you are . . .

A **college bookstore, a professor, an instructor, or work in higher education** and you'd like to place an order or request an exam copy, please contact jbreview@wiley.com.

A **general retail bookseller** and you'd like to establish an account or speak to a local sales representative, contact Melissa Grecco at 201-748-6267 or mgrecco@wiley.com.

An **exclusively on-line bookseller**, contact Amy Blanchard at 530-756-9456 or ablanchard @wiley.com or Jennifer Johnson at 206-568-3883 or jjohnson@wiley.com, both of our On-line Sales department.

A **librarian or library representative**, contact John Chambers in our Library Sales department at 201-748-6291 or jchamber@wiley.com.

A **reseller, training company/consultant, or corporate trainer**, contact Charles Regan in our Special Sales department at 201-748-6553 or cregan@wiley.com.

A **specialty retail distributor** (includes specialty gift stores, museum shops, and corporate bulk sales), contact Kim Hendrickson in our Special Sales department at 201-748-6037 or khendric@wiley.com.

Purchasing for the **Federal government**, contact Ron Cunningham in our Special Sales department at 317-572-3053 or rcunning@wiley.com.

Purchasing for a **State or Local government**, contact Charles Regan in our Special Sales department at 201-748-6553 or cregan@wiley.com.